The Diseases of Horses

Clarence B. Denny.

The Diseases of Horses,

THEIR

PATHOLOGY, DIAGNOSIS, AND TREATMENT;

TO WHICH IS ADDED

A COMPLETE DICTIONARY OF EQUINE
"MATERIA MEDICA."

By **HUGH DALZIEL**,
Author of "The Diseases of Dogs," &c.

LONDON:
L. UPCOTT GILL, 170, STRAND, W.C.

The Diseases of Horses.

INTRODUCTION.

VETERINARY science and its votaries are unfortunately not generally—in this country at least—held in the esteem, and have not attained to that position of popularity their importance and usefulness so justly deserve. We are the most conservative of people, and hold on alike to our "glorious constitution" and our "stupid prejudices" with the tenacity of our English bulldogs. Probably, as we have half swallowed the pill of compulsory education, and as it is sure to go down altogether with the jolting of time, the British owners of the unparalleled number—as shown by agricultural statistics—of over fifty millions of the finest stock the world can show, may in the course of another generation begin to question the propriety of a system of wholesale drugging at haphazard, and to doubt the wisdom of trusting the health and lives of their stock to the traditional ignorance and heirloom mysteries of the farrier, the ostler, and the cowman, instead of the skill of the trained veterinarian.

The honourable craft of horse doctoring has undergone many vicissitudes. In the earliest times medicine was studied and applied by the same practitioner to the relief of diseases of all animals associated with man as well as to man himself, and among the ancient writers of both Greece and Rome considerable advance was made in the study of veterinary science. But with the fall of the Roman empire this science, like others, fell into decay, and appears to have remained neglected for many centuries.

In, I believe, the fifteenth century, when the practice of shoeing horses with iron began to be more generally adopted, the practice of horse physic was revived, and was handed over to the farrier, or ferrier, or shoeing-smith, as the name implies, being taken from the Latin *ferrum* (iron). Such an inconsistency as making the shoemaker the doctor might be natural to the dark ages, but that it should be persevered in with unyielding stupidity by the intelligent British horse owner of the latter half of the nineteenth century is a mystery I leave others to solve, as it is incomprehensible to me. The fact, however, is unquestionable, that by the vast majority of stock owners, the qualified man is set aside in favour of the ignorant dealer in mystification, and the infallible trumpery of the empiric is preferred to modes of treatment and preparations the outcome of the united wisdom and research of the whole of our veterinary colleges. Such charges as these do not apply to the higher agricultural associations, nor generally to their individual members, but that they are true of the average English farmer, and the great majority of lesser owners, there are unfortunately too many proofs. This does not, I am sure, arise from a want of love for the horse, for nowhere is he held in such esteem or seen in such perfection. Our tight little island has always been famous for its horses; even the Romans, when they occupied England, found our native breed so superior as to be worth exporting to Rome, and since then, and especially since the time of King James I., what has not English skill and care done in improving this noble animal, that "gives profit to the poor and pleasure to the rich?" We have, indeed, produced an animal the acme of perfection, the envy of the world, an animal, in the words of an old writer, "with the courage of the lion, the fleetness of the deer, the strength of the ox, and the docility of the spaniel."

On our equine favourite we often lavish a vast expenditure, and spare no pains in bringing him to the highest condition, and to display his splendid form and noble qualities to the best advantage, and, in doing this, we are guided by the accumulated wisdom of an experience gained by a close and careful study of his nature and habits, and it is only when disease attacks him that common sense is put aside for faith in mystery. No doubt a vast deal of the injurious physicking to which the horse is subjected is undertaken with the best of intentions, but we all know which road is paved with these, and if the horse could speak, how often would he say "You may mean well, my master, but if you only knew the suffering you cause me, you would try and understand me better." Even poor Hodge, the waggoner, who stints himself of his beer and saves from his own spare pocket money to buy "vitriol" or some almost equally injurious "coating powders," to be given to his team on the sly, is prompted by the most laudable motives, and acts in pure but mistaken kindness to the animals under his charge, whom he wishes in his honest pride to excel his neighbours'; and in thus ignorantly drugging his horses he but follows the example set by his superiors. I do not expect by the little knowledge I can communicate on the subject to make any palpable difference in this respect, but as the weakest efforts when rightly directed do some good, I hope, if only by directing the attention of horse owners to a subject of such importance, to effect some alleviation in the unnecessary suffering of their animals, and that at a saving of cost to themselves.

It is not my intention to attempt to grapple with the more abstruse questions connected with the subject—which would indeed be valueless to the general reader—but to endeavour, as plainly as possibly, to enable those who wish to recognise the existence of disease to avoid the causes, and to select such remedies as may with safety and advantage be used in the hands of any intelligent man, and to point out such measures of home treatment as may mitigate suffering, and assist, instead of retarding, the operations of the veterinary surgeon, should it be necessary to call him in.

As in the book on "The Diseases of Dogs," I propose, for convenience of reference, to take the subjects in alphabetical order, instead of attempting a classification, which in this case, and for our simple purposes, would be useless and confusing. As it appears to me that every owner of stock to any extent should keep a collection of the most generally useful medicines by him, I will give a complete list of drugs used in treating the diseases of the horse, with their properties and doses, out of which the contents of a really useful horse medicine chest may be selected, *The Field* horse medicine chest, introduced to the public by me a few years ago, being open to some practical objections and capable of very great improvements.

I have already observed or implied, and I repeat, that the treatment of all serious and complicated cases of disease or injury should be left to the qualified veterinary surgeon, who by his special education, training, and practice is alone fitted to do so efficiently and without danger to the animal; but as we do not in our own cases run to the doctor on every slight occasion, no more is it necessary to call in the veterinarian when by attention to incipient symptoms and the timely use of simple and appropriate remedies disease may be warded off; and it is in the hope that in some degree, however slight, I may contribute to this end that I write.

In compiling the various articles I have laid under contribution the writings of the most advanced authorities on these subjects, but my object being to collect useful information, and convey it to amateur readers in the most simple language, except where a verbatim quotation is given, I have thought it unnecessary to make special reference to any one source, as it might equally apply to several.

A.

Abdomen, Diseases of.—The abdomen is the region or cavity of the belly containing the stomach, bowels, liver, bladder, &c., for diseases of which consult articles under those separate heads.

Abdomen, Wounds of.—(See *Wounds*.)

Abscess.—Abscess is the name given to a collection of pus or matter formed and deposited in some of the tissues of the body. It generally arises from a bruise or other injury, and its formation is always attended with increased heat of the part, and is so recognised, as also by pain and swelling. As it advances it becomes more localised, or comes to a head, when, if not opened, it will generally ulcerate and discharge through the skin. The danger in an abscess is that it should discharge internally, when death is the result; the object, therefore, is to stimulate the process and by hot fomentations, poultices, &c., to soften the skin and draw the matter towards the surface. When abscesses are deep-seated it is unsafe for anyone unaccustomed to the knife to attempt to open them; where they are more superficially situated they may by attention to a few general rules be safely and successfully treated. When first discovered, the part should be bathed with water as hot as can well be borne, and this must be kept up continuously—an intermittent application being worse than useless—or a poultice made with bran and hot water, and which cannot be too large, should be kept constantly applied, and changed as it gets at all cold. To prevent the evaporation of heat, cover it with woollen cloths when practicable. Sometimes when an abscess forms very tardily, it is advisable to apply a blister, or a good strong stimulating liniment should be rubbed all over the swelled part with considerable friction, and poultices afterwards applied. When the abscess is fully formed, or ripe, as it is called, which may be ascertained by its prominence, softness to the touch, and partial fluidity of its contents, it should be opened with an abscess knife or strong lancet, by inserting it into the softest and most prominent part and cutting downwards when the position will permit of that, so as to insure good and speedy drainage of the matter; pressure, and afterwards keeping the parts clean, is all that is then necessary, unless the wound shows an indisposition to heal, when it may be washed with a stimulating lotion, or the following ointment, which is useful for dressing any old sore that shows an indisposition to heal, may be applied a few times:

Ointment for Healing Wounds.—Take red precipitate, 2dr.; Venice turpentine, 1oz.; lard, 1oz., mixed.

If an abscess has been of such magnitude as to cause debility, the horse should have a course of tonic powders, which from their general utility we may at once introduce here.

Tonic Powders.—For debility, loss of appetite, emaciation, want of blood, wasting, &c.: Take pure sulphate of iron, 6oz.; powdered gentian root, 4oz.; powdered ginger, 2oz.; ground carraways, 3oz.; bicarbonate of soda, 1oz.; locust bean meal ½lb. Mix thoroughly and give a tablespoonful in the food (slightly damped) twice a day.

B.

Back Sinews, Strain or Sprain of.—This is one of the numerous injuries to which the complicated structure of the foot and leg are liable, and as with the horse " 'tis the pace that kills," so it oftenest happens to those put to fast work; and as these tendons support a good deal of the animal's weight when the foot comes to the ground in galloping or jumping they become strained. It also often happens to cart horses, especially those used on hilly roads, and to others that are constantly pushed beyond their natural pace. The flexor or bending tendons are inclosed in a sheath of cellular substance, for their greater protection, and by sudden or sustained over-exertion, this sheath gets injured by the pressure of the tendon, and if the injury be slight it may be confined to the sheath, and may exist some time without lameness, or so little as to be unobserved, or thought unworthy attention, but unless the horse has rest and attention it will be sure to get worse and worse, and end in permanent lameness.

In bad cases some of the ligamentous fibres get ruptured, whereby the inflammation is increased, and considerable lameness at once produced; in such cases the limb is flexed or bent, the horse endeavours to save the leg from having any weight, the toe only is put to the ground, and the local swelling, heat, and tenderness will plainly indicate the seat of the injury. In slighter cases of strain of the back sinews the horse shows the lameness most on first being taken out of the stable; and as it in some such instances disappears with moderate exercise, it has led to the belief that it can be worked off; but such a thing never occurs, and invariably, after standing a while, the lameness will be found to have returned, and without proper treatment and prolonged rest, it will get worse and worse.

In bad or repeated strains, and particularly when proper care has not been taken, stimulating liniments or other improper applications used, and when the horse has been again put to work before the parts have recovered their proper state, the sinews become shortened or contracted, the horse steps only on his toe, and the front of the fetlock comes almost, or entirely, to the ground, the joint being what is termed overshot. Preventive measures are, to a great extent, in every horse owner's and driver's hands, and the exercise of care, judgment, and humanity in using the horse, would, in a great majority of cases, at once save the animal from much suffering and his owner from pecuniary loss. Unfortunately, however, the willing beast is in too many instances treated with the utmost heartlessness, and used and valued merely as a steam engine or other machine, costing so much money, and to be made to realise so much at whatever cost of pain and suffering to the dumb brute. But, taking it on the lowest grounds, this system does not pay, for even a piece of mechanism like a steam engine cannot, with ultimate profit, be constantly driven at the highest pressure; how much less the finer and wonderfully complicated organism of the horse. It is so far satisfactory to reflect that Nemesis dogs the steps of inhumanity, but our friend and slave, the horse, deserves consideration on higher grounds, and it is ever true "the merciful man is merciful to his beast."

In attempting curative treatment in this, and, indeed in all similar accidents where inflammation is produced, there are some errors in domestic practice which it is necessary to refer to in order that they may be guarded against. It should be laid down as a rule, and adhered to, by all who have to do with horses and who attempt to treat them for such injuries, that neither blisters, stimulating liniments, nor hot, burning oils must be used whilst heat and tenderness of the part remain; these—except the last mentioned—will follow in due time, and if judiciously used, will strengthen the weakened parts; but if used during the inflammatory stage they do harm; yet how common do we find it that both in the stableman's and farmer's mind the most unalterable prejudice exists in favour of some famous oils, probably—as I know they often do—containing powerful mineral acids; or somebody's "celebrated liniment," which, though compounded of the most incongruous mess of incompatibles, is yet warranted to cure everything, from a sore shoulder to a break-down. All such things must be discarded, and reliance placed on simpler and more efficient means, combined with rest and home comfort to the animal.

In slight cases apply warm poultices of bran or linseed meal, renewing them as often as they get cold, or keep up continuous hot fomentations for several days, or as long as the place is hot and tender; plain water will answer the purpose as well as anything else; but if a prejudice exists in favour of "yerbs," such as marsh mallow, houseleek, &c., they can do no harm; and for the benefit of such I transcribe a very old recipe from Gervase Markham, one of the earliest English writers on veterinary subjects. He says for "any grief in his nether joints, whereby the horse goeth stiff and halteth, then take a handful of laurel leaves and of primrose leaves, of ground ivy, of crowfoot, of mallows, of red fennel, and of fine hay, of each of them severally as much; seethe them well together, and then let them stand fourteen days; then bathe the joint with it once a day, and bind of the herbs into it for four days together; then after chafe into the joint fresh grease and oil mixed together, and it will ease all his pain." Dr. Bracken, writing 150 years later, recommends as a "cold charge for strain of the back sinews—Bole Armenica ½lb., white wine vinegar, and white of eggs as much as will make it the consistence of a poultice—to be applied spread pretty thick on a piece of leather, and as it grows dry put more on." I have known very similar applications used in the present day.

In severe cases it may be necessary, the sooner to relieve and to prevent the inflammation extending and producing consequent derangement of the system, to bleed the horse. This may be done at the toe, and if necessary the bleeding may be encouraged by placing the foot in a bucket of warm water. When sufficient has been taken, and the bleeding stopped, the poultices or hot fomentations must be used, and continued till the inflammation subsides, which may be in two or three days. Cold applications should then be resorted to, such as vinegar and water in equal parts, with a wineglassful of spirit of wine added to every quart, or the following lotion will answer still better:

Lotion for Strain of Back Sinews.—Take of sal ammoniac, ½oz.; strong acetic acid, 3oz.; methylated spirits of wine, 2oz.; and water to make up a wine bottle.

The lotions must be applied by means of a bandage, which should be kept constantly wetted, this should be continued for several weeks, when the horse should be either fired or blistered, and allowed a considerable period of rest. Complete recovery from severe cases is not to be looked for, and, although the horse will recover sufficiently to be very useful, he should be afterwards kept to light and rather slow work, for if pressed or put to hard work lameness is very likely to recur.

It may be found useful in beginning the treatment to give the horse a dose of physic, and if the case has been neglected and the animal is feverish, he will also require some fever medicine; but this may be avoided by care and attention, particularly to his diet, which should, during treatment, consist of clover or cut grass, if obtainable, or roots, such as carrots or steamed potatoes with steamed corn, and the return to usual feed should be gradual, as inflammatory and feverish symptoms disappear.

Barbs and Paps.—The horse is furnished with a number of glands for the secretion of saliva, and these open and discharge the fluid by small protuberances underneath the tongue. The submaxillary glands open on each side of the bridle of the tongue, presenting a teat-like appearance, and in cases of cold, inflammation, &c., these swell and become tender, causing some difficulty in mastication; and in this swollen and inflamed state they form what are known as barbs or paps in the mouth. Old farriers recommend their excision, and the practice still prevails among the ignorant; and the immediate result of this cruel and stupid practice is that reduction of the local inflammation is produced by the bleeding, but the wound made is difficult to heal, the discharge of saliva helps to spread the sore, or the orifice of the duct gets closed, and the fluid it contains, finding no outlet, accumulates until it bursts, and a deep-seated ulcerous sore is formed beneath the tongue, which may puzzle the most skilful practitioner to cure. When we consider that these glands discharge into the mouth an amount of saliva absolutely necessary for the proper mastication of the food, the parotid alone discharging, on the authority of Youatt, a pint and a half an hour during mastication, the folly of tampering with them becomes apparent. The treatment really required is to remove the cause by giving a dose of physic and a few doses of cooling medicine, and at the same time to keep the animal on soft and easily masticated food; Walsh recommends in obstinate cases, that they be touched every second day with caustic, just at the opening of the duct. Similar enlargements of the opening of the sublingual glands, are known as gigs, bladders, and flaps.

Belly Ache.—See *Colic*.

Bladder, Inflammation of.—This is not of very frequent occurrence in the horse, and is probably often caused by the giving of cantharides as a stimulant; or it may arise from the presence of calculus or stone in the bladder; or it may be the result of a blow cruelly inflicted with the toe of a heavy boot; it may also exist as sympathetic with inflammation of the kidneys. The symptoms are irritability of the bladder shown by the frequent passing of urine in small quantities, and with considerable straining, and pain is evidenced by the animal often looking anxiously round towards its hind quarters. The horse should receive a dose of linseed oil sufficient to purge—a pint and a half, or two pints, and he should be well supplied with water, linseed tea, or thin gruel, and also with mashes of linseed and bran, the linseed being boiled or thoroughly scalded with boiling water so as to extract the mucilage; this treatment with rest will generally be all sufficient, but if the case is very severe, one of the following balls may be given every four hours :

Balls for Inflammation of the Bladder.—Take opium, 1½dr.; extract of belladonna, ½dr.; camphor, 1½dr.; made into a convenient sized ball with linseed meal and treacle.

Bladders.—See *Barbs*.

Bleeding.—So long as the Veterinary art was entirely in the hands of the farrier and the blacksmith, letting blood was the grand panacea for all the ills horseflesh is heir to; it was also held to be the great prophylactic or preventive of horse diseases, and with this idea the animals were regularly bled, spring and fall, and sometimes as often as four times a year, and to some extent the vicious system still prevails, and is held by many—at least their actions lead one to think so—as the universal remedy. Let a farrier be called in to see a horse, and no matter what ails him, if he is at all puzzled—which, as a matter of course, he generally is—the chances are a hundred to one that he will bleed him; this makes a show, has a palpable effect on the horse, covers the man's ignorance, and should the animal recover he gets great credit; whereas, should the horse die, how convenient it is to debit Providence with it, or, "Ah, if you had but sent for me sooner." No doubt there are urgent cases as in strong inflammation, when the prompt use of the fleam or the lancet is not merely of great benefit, but offers the only chance of saving life; but to open a vein and take away so much of the life of an animal should not be undertaken without due consideration, and those who in this matter plead the excuse that if it does no good it can do no harm are greatly mistaken. Periodical bleeding of healthy animals is not only uncalled for and useless, but, when persisted in, it begets a habit of body which makes the continued repetition of it imperative, and instead of warding off disease, as it is supposed to do, it but weakens the animal, laying him more open to the attacks of disease, and less able to resist their effects.

The instruments used in bleeding horses are the lancet, the fleam and the blood stick used for striking the fleam. The most usual place to bleed, when the general system is to be affected by the operation, is the jugular vein in the upper part of the neck, 4in. or 5in. from the fork where it divides and branches off. An expert operator would raise the vein by pressure with his finger; but it is a common practice to do so by tieing a string round the neck, the fleam must be placed on the vein longitudinally, the hair having been previously wetted and smoothed down so as to show it properly. It must then receive a stroke with the blood stick sufficient to cause it to cut through the skin and outer side of the vein; if the blow is too strong there is danger of cutting through the opposite side of the vein. The orifice should be sufficiently large to allow of a free and quick flow of blood. The vessel to receive the blood, and which should be properly marked, so that the quantity taken may be accurately known, must be pressed gently against the neck, and when the desired quantity has been taken it must be gently removed; and then the operator, taking hold of the lips of the wound with his finger and thumb, places them together and secures them in that position by passing a small pin through them by a very slight hold; the point of the pin is then nipped off and a little tow lightly twisted round it to secure it in its position. It is advisable to tie up the horse's head for a time. In the course of a few days the pin may be withdrawn. If the operation throughout is not skilfully performed there is a danger of the blood flowing beneath the skin and causing inflammation of the vein. This is known by heat and swelling of the part, which should be met by the application of the cooling lotion given at page 9. If not attended to it extends along the vein, the swelling increasing, and hard lumps arising, which will require the repeated use of blisters, one or two fever balls (p. 23) to be given, and the horse kept to light diet of mashes, &c. Should such untoward circumstances arise, the biniodide of mercury blister (p. 24) will be the most suitable application.

Bleeding is also practised from the thigh vein, frequently so for supposed shoulder lameness that does not exist. Farmers bleed from the palate for gripes and megrims; and, without a correct knowledge of the position of the veins, the practice is an unsafe one. In ophthalmia blood is taken from the vein just below the eye; and bleeding from the toe and coronet is practised for the relief of various affections and injuries to the feet and legs. In the latter cases it is often advisable to place the foot in a bucket of warm water to encourage the bleeding. No horse should be bled when suffering from abscess or unhealthy ulcers, as it tends to promote the absorption of the fluids and poison the blood. The quantity of blood to be taken from a horse must of course be regulated by circumstances, the strength and condition of the horse, and the degree of inflammation to be subdued. In some cases six quarts or more may be taken.

Blisters.—Blisters are used as counter-irritants in cases of internal inflammation and injury, with the view of setting up external inflammation, which is found to have the effect of relieving the internal parts that are suffering. After their application the skin or outer cuticle rises up in blots or blisters, filled with a watery substance—hence the name.

There are numerous drugs used as blistering agents, and the formulæ for making blisters are also exceedingly numerous. The needless multiplication of remedial agents of any class is to be deprecated, and far more so "ringing the changes" on the slightest variations of their compounds. Nearly every farrier, country druggist and stableman has his own form of blister kept a profound secret, and claiming to have special virtues of its own. These agents cannot be too simple in their composition; the more complicated they are the less likely are they to act effectually, and the more likely to create sores troublesome to heal. Euphorbium, once greatly in vogue amongst farriers is little, if at all, used by the veterinary surgeon, and the highly dangerous practice of adding white mercury (corrosive sublimate), and other mineral poisons cannot be too strongly condemned. The great vesicatory is cantharides, or Spanish fly. This is used mixed with fatty matter, or the active principle held in solution by various solvents, such as acetic acid, turpentine, olive oil, &c.; these are used of different strengths, according to the amount of irritation it is desired to produce. A mild form is the vinegar of cantharides, made by digesting one part by weight of flies in eight parts of diluted acetic acid, and filtering. A very useful mild blister is made as follows. It may be kept at hand of this strength when it can be easily increased, if needed, by the addition of more flies. It should be kept in a jar covered with bladder, and should be kept in a cool and dry place.

Mild Blister.—Take lard 6oz., beeswax 1oz., camphor 1oz., powdered cantharides 1oz.; melt the wax and lard with a gentle heat, and place in them the camphor, previously cut very small, or reduced to powder. Stir in the powdered cantharides, stirring occasionally till cold to ensure the ingredients being thoroughly mixed.

The biniodide of mercury blister is referred to in the article on bruises (p. 24).

In applying blisters to the horse the hair should be clipped off very short, and the blister rubbed in with considerable friction. If the part has been previously well fomented or poulticed, the action of the blister will be greatly assisted. In six or eight hours after the application vesication will have taken place, and on the following day the part should be carefully and tenderly freed from the irritating substance by bathing with warm water and a soft sponge; the part should then be dressed with some spermaceti ointment, fresh lard, or lead liniment made thus:

Lead Liniment.—Mix one part of extract of lead with five parts of best olive oil.

It is sometimes desired to keep a blister open. This can be done by dressing with savine ointment, or with a very mild preparation of cantharides.

Blood Spavin.—See *Spavin*.

Bloody Urine, or Passing of Blood.—This may be caused by calculus and sometimes by hard riding, causing rupture of one or more small vessels of the kidneys. At times it proceeds from ulceration in one of the urinary passages. The evidence of the disease is, of course, plain in the discoloured urine; this is passed without pain, and in many cases all the treatment required is to give the animal perfect rest. A mild dose of physic may be needed, and the diet should be light. If that is not found sufficient, a few of the following balls may be given at intervals of six or eight hours.

Balls for Bloody Urine.—Take acetate of lead 2dr., opium 1½dr., and tannic acid ½ dr., made into a ball with the common mass.

Bog Spavin.—See *Spavin*.

Bone Spavin.—See *Spavin*.

Bots.—These grubs, which infest all horses that have been turned out to grass in the summer or autumn months, have a very interesting history, which was first traced and made clear to us by the investigations of Mr. Bracy Clark; prior to his researches comparatively little was known of them, and a writer not much anterior to him speaks of them as being found only in the rectum and gut, which they never occupy but in passing through, when about to assume the chrysalis state. They were popularly supposed to be produced by bad food, and themselves again the cause of much mischief; such opinions are still common, and they are still a bugbear to those knowing nothing of their nature and history, and no doubt a person thus ignorant, on seeing a horse that had died of disease opened and dissected, and observing such large clusters of living bots as adhere to the stomach, might be pardoned for assuming that they were the cause of, or had something to do with, the cause of death, for doubtless to the superficial observer they look formidable and forbidding enough. When, too, in the early part of summer, as they are quitting their winter residence and passing through the body of the horse prior to undergoing their second metamorphosis, they are noticed by grooms in the dung, and adhering to the fundament; needless alarm is created, and all sorts of worm medicines are resorted to, to the great injury of the horse, but without having the slightest effect on the bots, although, from the fact of their leaving the horse at that time in obedience to nature, the medicine gets the credit of their expulsion, is supposed to have done a wonderful amount of good, and gets at once placed high in the catalogue of occult stable remedies. As bots, when first swallowed by the horse, attach themselves to the insensible cuticle coat of the stomach, where they remain and grow to maturity, they cause no irritation or inconvenience; and, as a matter of fact, the horse enjoys perfect health whilst clusters of them adhere to that part of his stomach. It therefore shows how useless it is to interfere; and more especially so as it has been abundantly proved that no known vermifuge has any effect in dislodging them, but that there they remain till their appointed season of migration. We should not, therefore, attempt what is impossible, and would be useless if accomplished, especially as medicines given for such a purpose are more or less injurious to the horse, and in some cases, as when savin, tobacco, and other powerful drugs are resorted to, highly dangerous.

This will be better understood and appreciated if we give a short sketch of the history of the species of gadfly (*Œstrus equi*) of which the bot is the grub or larva. In the latter part of summer these flies may be observed very busy about the horses out at grass. The female fly darts about the foreparts of the horse, poises herself in the air, and prepares to deposit an egg on the selected part. This is done with great quickness, the egg being left on a hair, to which it is secured by a glutinous liquor which soon dries. The operation is repeated again and again, and on one horse there will sometimes be deposited from four to five hundred of these eggs. Those parts only of the horse are chosen that can be easily reached with his tongue, the insides of the knees, points and sides of shoulders, being commonly selected. The eggs are hatched, or ripe for hatching, in a few days, and as the horse licks himself, which he is the more inclined to do from the teazing of the flies, his warm, moist tongue opens the egg, and liberates a small, lively worm, which gets carried with the food into the stomach, if fortunate enough to escape the grinders —for, of course, numbers must perish this way. On reaching the stomach they attach themselves by means of two little hooks or tentacles with which they are provided, one on each side of the mouth, to the white coat of the stomach; here they remain in clusters, firmly fixed, feeding on the mucus of the stomach during the autumn, winter, and spring months. In the early or middle part of summer they voluntarily leave their stronghold, and are discovered by the groom or attendant in considerable numbers as they pass with the dung. They now assume the chrysalis state, and, circumstances being favourable to their development, in four or five weeks each becomes a perfect fly. These mate together, the females deposit their eggs, and so the same wonderful round of changes go on, and the species is perpetuated.

It will be seen from this that no horse that had not been out at grass the previous summer will have the bots. To this there may be a few rare exceptions, as the gadfly might find the horse in the stable or the fold, or the horse might lick the eggs off a companion brought in from grass. It is generally, if not universally, held by those best capable of forming an opinion on the subject, that bots are harmless to the horse. It is also agreed that it is impossible, by worm medicines, to dislodge them from their hold on the stomach; for, as has been truly observed, you may push poison down the horse's throat, but you cannot compel the worms to take it, and, therefore, we ought not to torture the horse and risk injuring his constitution by vain attempts at the useless and the impossible.

Break Down.—There has been considerable difference of opinion as to what constitutes break down, and a good deal of confusion still exists in many minds; severe sprain of the back sinews being called by many horsey men, and also by numbers of professional writers, break down. But by the more recent writers on these subjects the term is now applied to a rupture of the suspensory ligament. This accident usually occurs to tired-out horses at the end of a hard gallop, or in the last few strides of a race—the fetlock and pastern joints lose their support, and the fetlock is let down till it bears on the ground. Perfect recovery is not to be looked for, but the animal may be sufficiently patched up to be useful in slow farm work. The treatment should consist in at once applying hot poultices or fomentations, succeeded by cooling lotions, blistering, or firing, and turning the horse out to grass for a summer. In fact, the same treatment as recommended for sprain of the back sinows should be followed here. It is by many recommended to make the horse wear a high-heeled shoe, as a measure of relief; and in every case long and perfect rest is indispensable to even partial recovery.

Brittle Hoof.—This is a state of the hoof frequently causing great inconvenience, it is so hard and brittle that pieces often chip off whilst the horse is being shod. It is not an infrequent cause of sand-crack, and although this sort of hoof appears to be natural to some animals, it is more generally the result of neglect. When it exists extra care in shoeing is required, as it is often so thin as to make the danger of pricking and consequent lameness imminent. The application of water is to be avoided, because, although it makes the hoof softer at the time, it becomes harder and more brittle and shelly afterwards.

One of the best preparations to remedy this state of the hoof, prevent sandcrack, and vastly increase the growth of hoof in all cases where weak and shelly, is the preparation known as "Dalziel's Hoof Ointment," being one of the articles in "The Field Horse Medicine Chest" as prepared by me, the recipe for making which is as follows, and can be readily made by anyone:

Dalziel's Hoof Ointment.—Barbadoes tar, 12oz., beeswax, 12oz., mutton suet, 12oz., and yellow rosin 4oz.

In making, procure a suitable jar in which you intend to keep the ointment, and into it place first the rosin and wax, broken up tolerably small, because these require more time to melt than the other ingredients, place in the oven, and when pretty nearly melted add the suet, and, when all three are dissolved, the Barbadoes tar. When taken out of the oven it must be constantly stirred till cold to insure thorough incorporation of ingredients. The hoof should be regularly dressed with this, especially in wet weather, when the horse should never leave the stable without having it first applied. Having washed and dried the hoof, partially melt the top of the ointment and apply it freely with a brush, rubbing it in well, and where the hoof is very thin and weak the horse should wear a leather sole, and having melted a portion of the ointment, it should be poured in warm at the heels. Anyone whose horse requires such treatment, and will give the above a month or two of trial, will be agreeably surprised with the result.

Broken Knees.—These are probably of more frequent occurrence than any other accident to the horse. Some horses, by their conformation, are more liable to them than others of a better shape. The animal with thick and upright shoulders and legs standing far under him, and with a short, pottering movement, is more likely to be the possessor of broken knees than one with good oblique shoulders, high withers, and strong forearm. Accidents, however, will happen to the best of horses, particularly if ridden or driven carelessly; and, again, the rider or driver who is always jerking at bridle or reins, and who cuts with a whip for a stumble— as unavoidable as if the wiseacre had stumbled himself—is quite as likely to " throw the horse down " as the most careless. Such accidents are of grave importance, as they often cause unsightly blemishes and permanent injuries, greatly reducing the value of the horse, and sometimes rendering him almost or entirely useless. There is no end to the gradations of injury thus inflicted, and when the fall results in a clean cut of the skin only, nothing is to be feared; and after sponging with luke-warm water to remove any dirt that may possibly have lodged in the cut, the skin can be drawn or rather pressed together till the two lips of the wound exactly meet, and kept so by a few strips of sticking plaster. If this is done neatly and well no blemish will be left discoverable by ordinary examination, and in such a case the animal would not be a pin the worse practically. Bruises, which may injure the bones, and contused wounds, are the greatest source of danger. As the horse falls on his knees, the force with which he was going carries him along the ground, and if the road is hard the skin is severed, and the lower lip of the wound in scraping along collects sand and grit, and as he rises the elasticity of the skin brings it back and forms a pouch which holds the dirt, and from which it is most difficult to remove it; if the joint is injured by the capsular ligament being penetrated, so as to permit of the escape of synovia or joint-oil, the injury is indeed serious. On the occurrence of the accident the horse should, as soon as possible, be quietly led to the stable, and there, with the utmost gentleness, the extent of the injury should be examined into. To effect this object the first thing to do is to remove all foreign bodies, as gravel, sand, and dirt, and this is best effected, not by direct application of the sponge to the tender wound, but by the water out of it by pressure on the leg above the hurt, and thereby washing or swilling away the dirt without giving needless pain. The water used should be lukewarm, as cold water would tend to leave a larger and more apparent scar. A large poultice should next be applied and renewed when cold, on which, when taken off, the joint oil will be seen as a glairy yellowish transparent fluid, should the joint have been opened by the accident. In such a case the skilled veterinary surgeon should be at once consulted, who will take the proper means to close the orifice, and stop the flow of synovia, which lubricates the joints, and prevents the bones from grating against each other, which, if permitted, would cause inflammation of the delicate membrane which covers them. If the examination shows that the injury is not of so severe a character, the poultices may be continued for a day, and afterwards apply arnica lotion, of the strength of one ounce of tincture of arnica to a pint of cold water, keeping the knee constantly wetted till granulation takes place, after which the wound should be dressed once or twice a day with the following:

Lotion for Broken Knees.—Take crystal carbolic acid, 1dr.; glycerine, 15dr.; water, 2oz.; mixed to form a lotion.

In cases where the skin has been ruffled or puckered by dragging along the ground, and a pouch or bag formed, suspected of retaining dirt, Mayhew recommends the insertion of a seton at the lower part of it, to form a drainage for the escape of the foreign irritating bodies.

In no case of broken knees should officious knowing persons be permitted to probe the wound or inject strong stimulating or caustic fluids; this, ignorant ostlers and farriers are sometimes permitted to do, and even oil of vitriol has been used in such cases—such treatment is not only most injurious, but cruel and barbarous in the extreme. When the wound is healing, should proud flesh appear it may be kept down by dusting with powdered sulphate of copper (blue stone), but if the carbolic acid lotion is used as prescribed, this is not likely to be needed. The horse should at first be racked up, and if the blister is afterwards used as recommended, he should wear a cradle to prevent him gnawing. The comfort of the animal suffering from injury should be specially attended to, both on the grounds of humanity and as a means of cure; the feed should be light, consisting of mashes, steamed corn, and chaff, with roots, clover, or vetches, as the season and circumstances afford. After the wound is healed the blemish left will be diminished if the hair is taken off all round for some inches and the place blistered with the following:

Hair Stimulant.—Red iodide of mercury ointment—this is made by mixing one part of red or biniodide of mercury with ten parts of lard or resin ointment.

In using this ointment, it should be rubbed in with considerable friction, but not long enough to cause blistering, and it will be found to increase the growth of hair, moreover, the new hair will be all of one shade of colour, so that the blemish will be less noticeable. There are many other things in use to cause the hair to grow, tincture of iodine is sometimes used for this purpose, and gunpowder, mixed with lard, is a common application, but it can only help to conceal the blemish by colouring the part. The following ointment will, sometimes, have a good effect, but it must be remembered that where the roots of the hair have been destroyed it is impossible to make hair grow:

Camphor Hair Stimulant.—Powdered camphor, 2 drs.; powdered cantharides, 1 dr.; mild mercurial ointment, 2oz.; mixed, and a little well-rubbed in twice a day.

I believe, however, the red iodide of mercury will be found to be the best hair stimulant.

Broken Wind.—Of all classes of suffering animals claiming the sympathy of the humane perhaps none are so much to be pitied as the broken winded horse—past the prime of life, and suffering from a painful and incurable disease, too often the result of the ignorance or wantonness of the master to whom he has given the services of his best days; for it is astonishing how ignorance, prejudice, and passion, blind us to our best interests, even in money matters, and perhaps in few instances is this so strongly marked as in the treatment of the lower animals. The comparatively ruined horse at the very time when he requires the gentler treatment, easier work, and greater care which long and willing service would seem to have purchased the right to, is handed over for a money consideration to a new owner, whose greed or whose need urges him to force out of the poor beast, by whip or spur or angry voice, the utmost exertions that abused nature has left him the power of yielding at a cost of pain and suffering as incalculable as it is unheeded by the thoughtless, the cruel, and the ignorant. That excellent Society for the Prevention of Cruelty to Animals has done much to hinder cruelty and assuage the sufferings of horses, but their officers are not ubiquitous, nor are their powers all-reaching; nor, indeed, has fear of the law such power to prevent suffering as a correct knowledge of the animal's constitution, requirements, and capabilities gives, producing, as it does, a rational system of feeding and general treatment, resulting in his increased usefulness, the prevention of disease incapacitating to work, and, in consequence, adding at once to the master's profits and the horse's comfort. There are, however, those who will not be taught, and whose brutality can only be curbed by the dread of punishment. To such the poet's words apply—

> The fear of hell's the hangman's whip
> To keep the wretch in order,

and, therefore, for the repression of the incorrigibly cruel, those too brutish in nature to appreciate a system of kindness, and too blindly stupid to see that cruelty to their beast is ultimate loss to themselves, and that to grind out the life and energies of their horse at an unknown and unconsidered amount of suffering, treating it as though it were an inanimate machine, is penny wise and pound foolish. A broken winded horse is not such an accession to the stable as to make any person desirous of owning him, and no man would care to drive one who could afford a sound one, if at all ambitious to excel in horse flesh, but a fair plea may be urged that where a number are kept and one has become diseased in this way, a few pounds should not be allowed to outweigh all other considerations, and that, if slow, suitable work can be found for him, he should be retained rather than be handed over to the tender mercies of the dealer, or of those who will work the life out of him with no other feeding or intention than to make as much out of him as possible, *while he lasts*. There are the stronger reasons for this because, by proper feeding and judicious use, putting to slow and light work for which such a horse is alone fitted, together with proper palliative medicines, the animal will retain a great measure of usefulness, and more than earn his corn for many years; indeed, by patient and persistent treatment in the proper course he may be vastly improved, although r. t fully reinstated in his former health and usefulness. I have used the masculine gender, although mares are said to be more subject to this disease than horses, and young animals are but seldom sufferers, the aged, overworked, and ill-fed, and ill-stabled being the victims. Whether or not it is originally a disorder of the digestive organs, as maintained by some, the system of feeding is certainly often an inducing cause, and long compulsory subsistence on poor, innutritious food, compelling the animal to keep his stomach constantly on the stretch in order to obtain sufficient sustenance, is a common cause. It should always be remembered by those who have the management and feeding of horses that the stomach of that animal is remarkably small for his size, being in this respect a perfect contrast to the ox, whose capacious paunch may be always distended with food, his motions being slow, and who, in fact, seems to have nothing else to do than to eat and grow fat. Long continued feeding on dry food, as meal, bran, and dusty chaff and hay, may produce broken wind, as it aggravates it when established. The disease may be of slow growth, succeeding to chronic cough or cold, or to thick wind, &c., or brought on by persistent errors in feeding conjointly with unwholesome, ill-ventilated stabling; but it is also often caused suddenly, and this is generally so if, when the horse has been blown out with green food, or after a full feed of any kind, or a bucket of water, he is at once driven fast or put to heavy draught, and of course, the fuller the feed and the sharper the pace, the heavier the draught or the greater the exertion, whatever it may be, the greater the danger ; as in such a case the full, distended stomach, interferes with the increased action of the lungs, preventing the complete expulsion of the air; some of the air cells of the lungs become gorged, are ruptured, and run into each other; these unnatural cells retain the inhaled air, the forcible expulsion or attempt at expulsion of which causes ever after the double effort of expiration so characteristic of broken wind.

The symptoms of broken wind are so clearly marked that no disease is more easily recognised. The animal suffers from a short, grunting cough, which is forced out with a jerky, painful effort. Respiration is divided into three acts instead of two, as in health. The breath is drawn in quickly, and with a single effort ; expiration is broken into two distinct endeavours to expel the air, the first by the muscles used for that purpose in an ordinary state of health; these failing to do so entirely, the auxiliary muscles, more markedly those of the abdomen, come into play, rising to assist in emptying the lungs. These two efforts are slow and laboured and before completion the animal again requires to inhale fresh air; the muscles of expulsion suddenly relax, and the flank falls in with peculiar force, so as to catch the eye of the least observant. The double action in expiration and falling in of the flank are most marked characteristics of the disease, which cannot escape the notice of anyone. Other attendant symptoms frequently, if not always present, are a ravenous appetite and great thirst. Flatulence is also a troublesome and annoying accompaniment of broken wind; whilst the coat, which in so many cases quickly indicates a change in health, looks ragged and dirty, and the whole aspect of the animal is dejected. When driven fast, or the strength overtaxed, the nostrils distend, the breathing becomes more laboured and difficult, and the animal gives evidence of great distress.

To put such a horse to any other than slow and easy work is refined torture, which every thinking person with any pretensions to humanity will be ashamed to inflict. What would be thought of compelling a man suffering from asthma to run for miles at his utmost speed, or to wheel heavily weighted barrows, requiring the putting forth of his greatest strength, under the influence of the lash or the goad, applied heedless of his sufferings? Yet that is the treatment the equine sufferer is too often subjected to.

Prevention is in all cases better than cure, and most cases of broken wind may be prevented by sensible treatment. Let the stable correspond to the requirements of a healthy state, in cleanliness, ventilation, and general comfort; let his food be in form and quality such as his organisation and the demands on his services require; and never ride or drive him whilst his stomach is distended with food or water—even if compelled to travel, time will be gained by giving time for digestion as well as eating—or at least let his pace be of the slowest, rather than inflict such a misery on the beast, and thereby destroy the value of your own property.

Horses that have been out on rich pasture or clover should not be galloped, nor are these animals capable of sustaining a fast pace without danger to the wind; a horse to gallop far must be in a trained condition.

The reason that gentlemen's horses do not suffer from broken wind as those of farmers and others do, is not only that, being more highly bred, they are of a class less liable to it, but also that they are better stabled, better groomed, and generally fed, and otherwise treated on more rational principles. I am not aware that there is any cure for broken wind, although, of course, in such a tempting field many are the pretenders who say their nostrums will do so. The measures to be adopted in such cases are therefore palliative, and these, if persisted in, will keep the animal useful whilst relieving his sufferings.

As already said, the horse must not be put to fast or heavy work; feed six times a day when convenient, instead of three or four times—that is, divide the usual four feeds into six; let the food be of the best quality, and the principal part of it in a concentrated form, consisting of oats and beans, bran, and good cut straw, the whole slightly damped; in addition, sliced carrots or other roots, with a small proportion only of good hay, given morning and evening. Where the horse has not water *ad libitum*, it should be given in smaller quantities and at more frequent intervals than is usual under ordinary circumstances.

As an aid to digestion, the following powders may be occasionally resorted to with advantage:

Tonic Digestive Powders.—Take pure sulphate of copper in fine powder, 2oz.; powdered gentian root, 2oz.; powdered ginger, 2oz.; powdered liquorice root, 4oz.; powdered carraways, 6oz. To be thoroughly mixed and divided into sixteen powders, one of which to be given, sprinkled over the corn, once a day, the whole being slightly damped.

The list of drugs given with a view of directly alleviating or curing the disease is too long to enumerate; all medicines given for pneumonia, coughs, colds, &c., are used, including antimony, nitre, foxglove, belladonna, opium, &c.; whilst others are given with a view to act more immediately through the digestive organs.

The following ball, the prescription of a practitioner of very high standing in his profession, I have made for a long time, and have found of great value and much approved by many who have used it in cases of chronic cough, thick wind, roaring, whistling, and for the alleviation of broken wind. It is the broken-wind ball of "The '*Full*' Horse Medicine Chest," and is made as follows :

Ball for Broken Wind.— Take extract of belladonna, 3drs.; powdered squills, 1½oz.; camphor, 3drs.; common mass, 4oz. mix. A little powdered gum may be added, to make a more adhesive mass.

The belladonna, camphor, and squills should first be very carefully mixed, and then thoroughly incorporated with the common mass to ensure equal distribution of the active ingredients. The mass must then be divided into six equal sized balls; each ball must then be first wrapped up in a small piece of soft thin paper and again in a piece of tin foil, as the camphor, being a volatile oil, would soon evaporate. It is as well to keep the whole wrapped in oiled paper and in a cool and dry place. When administered, the tin foil must be removed, and the ball given in the thin paper. One occasionally will relieve, and one may be given daily for a time in severe cases with great effect, attention being at the same time given to the proper system of feeding.

Common Mass.—Common mass, referred to in the foregoing formula, is a mixture of equal parts of linseed meal and treacle, but any simple substance may be used instead, to form the active ingredients into a convenient-sized ball.

Unprincipled dealers and others sometime attempt and succeed in passing off a broken-winded horse as sound, and, to aid their nefarious practices, charge the animal's stomach with lard, shot, and other rubbish, which has the effect for a time of allaying the symptoms of the disease and deceiving the unwary. The temporary effect of such practices soon passes, and a pail of water to the suspected horse would speedily bring the hidden evil to light. Horse buyers should be on their guard against such frauds, and it is better in most cases to trust to the opinion of a qualified veterinarian on questions of soundness; the small fee charged is generally a good investment.

Bronchitis.—Bronchitis is an inflammation of the bronchial tubes or air passages communicating with the lungs. The mucous membrane lining the tubes is charged with blood, contracting the passage, thereby rendering the breathing more difficult, and in order to supply the lungs with the necessary quantity of fresh air, making it more rapid. The causes are the same as produce common cold, neglected cases of which frequently result in bronchitis, and that again extends to the lungs. Horses kept standing exposed in cold stormy weather, after a sharp run, till they get chilled, run a great risk of contracting bronchitis; and the traveller who pulls up half numbed with cold, where the cheerful blaze of the window invites a call, has, when seated before a roaring fire, with something comforting to the inner man steaming before him, a strong temptation to forget rather too long the faithful servant outside; but the practice is dangerous, and wanting in that care which the horse is entitled to. Bronchitis is rather an insidious foe, and, except with the groom, who is often an acute and careful observer, may take up a strong position unnoticed, or at least unheeded.

It frequently begins in the nasal passages, extending down the windpipe towards the lungs. There is running at the nose as an early symptom, and the inside of the nostrils is slightly inflamed and of a scarlet hue; the breathing is increased in rapidity, and to these symptoms is added a slight short cough. The appetite may be but little affected at first, and so long as the animal eats it is often presumed that nothing ails him; but the slightest change or falling off in appetite should be noted and the cause considered, and when accompanied by cough and increased discharge from the nostrils it should lead to closer observation and minute inspection. A fever ball, a few mashes, and steaming by means of the nosebag may at this early stage prevent much future mischief, and, indeed, restore the horse to its usual health. If the disease goes on unchecked, the appetite entirely fails, the breathing becomes still more rapid, and the breath is hot; the discharge from the nose becomes purulent and offensive; the cough becomes more severe and painful as the sufferer endeavours to force out the clotted mucus which threatens to choke him; the pulse is very much increased, and on auscultation—that is, listening to the breathing by placing the ear against the side—an unnatural wheezing and gurgling sound is heard; the countenance of the horse has a haggard expression, and he shows a disinclination to move. As an additional evidence of the true character of the disease, the legs and surface of the body will be found to be of uneven temperature.

In these cases it is a hopeful sign when the cough changes from the hard and suppressed and becomes looser, and the animal succeeds in discharging the accumulated mucus that had threatened to block up the passage to the lungs; and to assist and bring about this is the object to which we should direct our efforts.

As this is a quickly lowering disease, blood letting must be resorted to with extreme caution; although it may be desirable to do so at the onset of the attack, but the patient will not bear the loss of much blood. In treating bronchitis it is very important that the horse should have plenty of fresh air without creating a draught, and a good roomy loose box is the most suitable place for him. If the air can conveniently be rendered warm and humid by evaporation of water it will be of great service, but this if done must be kept up night and day. Failing this, get a long and deep nose bag, and, putting into the bottom of it a good quantity of bran and sweet hay cut fine, keep up a constant steaming by pouring boiling water over it as often as it gets at all cold, and every three hours rub well in boiling water 2dr. of the extract of belladonna and pour into the nose bag, the steam from which will allay the irritation in the windpipe and give great relief. At the outset the bowels should be acted on by a dose of linseed oil, and one of the following balls must be given night and morning:

Fever Balls.—Take tartarised antimony 1dr., camphor 1dr., and nitrate of potash 2dr. made into a small ball with common mass (p. 21).

The horse may also have every few hours 1oz. of laudanum mixed with 1oz. spirit of sulphuric ether, given in warm water or gruel. Blisters should be resorted to as soon as the existence of the inflammation is ascertained, and must be applied over the brisket and along the windpipe to the larynx; the mild blister given on page 12 must in this case be increased in strength by the addition of more cantharides, and the speedy action insured by thoroughly fomenting the part with warm water previous to applying the blister, which must be used, and the parts treated as advised under that head.

Bronchitis sometimes leaves behind it a chronic cough and a tenderness of the parts, rendering the horse specially sensitive to changes of temperature and exposure to wet and cold weather. For such cases the following form of cough ball is well suited:

Cough Ball.—Take powdered digitalis 1scr., camphor 1dr., nitrate of potash 1dr., powdered gum ammoniacum 2dr., Barbadoes tar 2dr., linseed meal 2dr., made into one ball.

One of these may be given as circumstances dictate, as often as night and morning if needed. As the horse returns to health he must be treated with great care and caution, both as to exposure to cold and in feeding, and dusty hay or chaff must be specially avoided. All food should be given moist for a time, the return to dry corn being very gradual, gruel mashes and boiled roots being made the staple food till health is restored. The balls prescribed should be made as small as possible that they may be the more easily given.

Bruises or Contusions.—These terms are used to describe external injuries caused by a fall, kick, or blow, when the skin is not lacerated; they are characterised by more or less swelling and heat of the part, and their effect is to obstruct the circulation, and in a greater or less degree destroy, for the time being, the vitality of the part. Bruises vary much in degree, and slight cases are easily managed, requiring only hot fomentations or poultices, succeeded by rubbing the part gently with a stimulating liniment, such as the following.

Stimulating liniment for Bruises, &c.—Take, turpentine, 4oz.; camphor, ½oz.; olive oil, 4oz.; spirit of hartshorn, 3oz.; oil of origanum, ½oz. Mix and keep well corked, and in a cool place, ready for emergencies. It should be plainly labelled, "For external use only."

The application of this liniment after the warm fomentation or poultice causes the absorption of effused blood, and reinstates the injured part in its ordinary condition. An application of spirit and water, or arnica lotion, would tend to the same end.

In more severe bruises a tumour may be formed and suppuration take place, which must be treated as an abscess, by poultices and warm fomentations, to bring it to a head, when it should be opened with a lancet, the matter pressed out, and the part kept clean to assist in healing. Bruises from blows or kicks on any bony part are apt to produce an indurated or hardened substance, which can only be reduced by treating with blisters, and for such a purpose the biniodide of mercury ointment is the most suitable. It is made thus:

Biniodide of Mercury Blisters.—Mix one part of red or biniodide of mercury with seven parts of lard, or, what is better, being rather harder, spermaceti or resin ointment. This ointment is identical with blisters, sold by various makers as secret proprietary remedies, at an enormous price.

In applying it considerable friction must be used, and when the parts become too tender to permit this, as shown by the vesicular eruption which it produces, its use should be abstained from for a few days till these effects have passed off, when it should again be resorted to till the desired result is attained. In some cases the ointment requires to be reduced in strength, where the skin is more than usually susceptible to irritation by it. This can easily be done by adding a little more lard. By its great influence in stimulating and facilitating absorption, this ointment is most serviceable in all cases of thickening of the integument, curbs, splents, incipient spavin, &c., and should be kept by all large horse owners.

When a bruise is of a very severe character, there is danger of the local inflammation extending and producing general disturbance of the system, and where this danger is imminent the diet should be of a non-stimulating nature; reduce the amount of corn, give some cut grass, clover, or vetches, and a few mashes with sliced carrots, if convenient. A dose of physic may also be given with advantage, and the horse may have four or six drachms of nitre in his water or mash for a few nights. These means, with the local applications advised, and such rest as the nature of the case shows to be expedient, will prove successful in preventing extension of the injury and removing local effects.

C.

Canker.—Canker is often the sequel to neglected or improperly treated cases of grease or thrush, and rarely or never occurs in horses properly attended to and kept in clean stables, but where they are compelled to stand in a filthy puddle of manure canker and other troubles are very likely to be the result. It is a kind of fungoid growth spreading over the sensitive frog and sole, ulcerating and discharging a foul and offensive matter. It is difficult to cure, and the first step to that end must be the removal of any exciting cause by attention to thorough cleanliness—all decomposed horn should be cut away and the ulcers exposed, so that they may be within reach of the proper remedies; the parts should then be touched with butyr of antimony, and a good dressing of the following applied on a piece of tow:

Dressing for Canker.—Take red precipitate one part, blue stone in fine powder four parts, lard twelve parts—or the two powders well mixed may be dusted over the sores and a pledget of tow applied.

As pressure is of importance the tow must be folded evenly and applied firmly, being kept in position by two thin pieces of iron crossing each other and slipped in under the shoe. The discharge should not be allowed to accumulate under this, but the foot must be examined, cleaned, and re-dressed at least every other day, and at each examination all loose and sloughing parts must be carefully cut away, keeping a perfectly level surface that the pressure may be equal.

Capped Hock and Capped Elbow or Capulet.—This is an injury to the point of the hock or elbow, causing enlargement, a degree of stiffness, and sometimes lameness. When observed, the whole hock joint should be examined to see how far the injury extends. It is generally the result of a blow, self-inflicted when the horse kicks in the stable, or it may be caused by the movement of the horse lying without proper bedding The amount of swelling varies considerably, as does the inflammation present. Situated just beneath the skin at these points are sacs, called *bursa mucosa*, lined with synovial membrane, for the lubrication of the tendons passing over the points of the bones; these get bruised, swell, and become soft and puffy to the feel, and the reduction of these to their natural condition is the object to be attained. The insertion of a seton below the swelling has been recommended and often tried, but the result is not satisfactory, and is to be avoided. The constant application of a cooling lotion, especially if resorted to in good time, is the safest and most generally successful treatment. A recipe for cooling lotion has already been given (p. 9), but if that is not handy do not wait till you can get it, but apply cold water at once, and this will be improved by adding a fourth part of good vinegar, or an eighth part of spirits, as whisky, brandy, &c. As has already been insisted on when cold lotions are applied, it is important the part should be kept cold by frequent application of fresh lotion, for the cloth or sponge with which they are used soon becomes hot when in contact with an inflamed surface. In these cases there is a difficulty in keeping the lotion at the place, from the point sticking out, but this can be overcome by making a bag in shape like a filter bag, and tying it above and below the joint. Fill the bottom with sponge, saturated with lotion, and leave a hole in the top side of the bag to pour in fresh supplies by, and so keep up the evaporation from the part. Where the case has been neglected it may be necessary to apply iodine. The cold lotions are only of use in the early stage. The hair may be cut close and the skin painted daily with compound tincture of iodine, or a weak ointment of biniodide of mercury (p. 17) may be used.

Cataract.—This is an affection of the eye of a serious nature, very frequently ending in blindness. It is known by different names, as capsular cataract, lenticular cataract, &c., according to the part of the eye affected. The pupil of the eye, which is a clear crystalline substance of jelly-like consistence, and convex in shape, is surrounded by a transparent sac or capsule; this becomes affected by inflammation of adjacent parts, and a deposit of lymph takes place, and the eye presents to an accurate observer a cloudy and rather mottled appearance; when this is caused by inflammation the other eye is apt to become affected also, whereas, if from the effects of a blow, the disease does not usually extend to the second organ. Cataract also arises from obscure constitutional causes, and in confirmed lenticular cataract the lens presents a pearly appearance, and one or more white opaque spots may be seen, varying in size from the head of a pin upwards. The disease may exist some time, and escape the observation of master and groom, and requires close inspection for the inexperienced to detect it; when suspected to exist, it will be best examined by leading the horse to the stable door, where there is a strong light, and looking closely into the eye sideways. The first symptoms that generally appear, and lead to the suspicion of the existence of cataract, is the horse becoming timid and shying, especially if he has not before shown a disposition to shy—not that every shying horse has a cataract, but the defective vision produced by its existence is a source of great danger, even worse than blindness, as the horse sees objects in a distorted form, impressing him with fear, and causing him to start aside even from objects with which he has been familiar. The causes of cataract are often obscure and unexplained, but sometimes result from inflammation of the conjunctiva, and sometimes the result of a blow. Mayhew ascribes this and other affections of the visual organs in some cases to the keeping of the horses' eyes constantly fixed on a whitewashed wall, as is the case in some stables, and points out how unnatural this is, and how painful and productive of evil, and requests his readers to prove it on themselves by holding up a sheet of white paper before their eyes for only half an hour. There is, no doubt, much truth in this; and any of my readers who have been out a day when the ground was completely covered with snow will know how painful it is to the eyes. All causes of inflammation will be avoided if we would avoid cataract, and heated and foul stables are … dly, or perhaps, more correctly, certainly, a prolific source of this disease. The strong and pungent smell of ammonia from decaying urine and manure allowed to collect in some ill-ventilated stable, spring… should warn the horse owner that the health on his horse is … by such emanation. For cataract there is no cure or remedy… the aqueour … with safety and propriety adopt, except in excess… in a slow inflammation therefrom, when … a … spring water, with an ounce of laudanum to a pint may be useful. Avoid the causes by order and cleanliness in the stable, and ensure abundance of fresh air by the adoption of a suitable system of ventilation; and in all cases, whilst providing plenty of light, do not let it be glaring, but have the walls of a subdued colour. In cases of doubt, in this as in all other equine diseases, consult a qualified veterinary surgeon.

Catarrh.—In its simple form catarrh or common cold is very easily managed, but as serious consequences arise from its neglect the first symptoms should receive prompt attention. Catarrh is attended with a slight deflux or discharge from the nose, and to this horses are very liable, because, unlike man, he breathes only through the nose, for which reason the nostrils are formed very wide, and the air passages are thereby somewhat more directly exposed to the consequences of sudden change or any other cause producing irritation of their lining membranes. As a cold unchecked is apt to extend to the larynx, bronchial tubes, and lungs, it becomes very necessary to be on guard and adopt precautionary measures to prevent such serious consequences. The appearance of the inside of the nose, especially of the septum—that is, the membrane which divides the nostrils—is such a delicate index of danger, threatened or existent, that most writers lay great stress on the importance of horse owners making themselves thoroughly familiar with its healthy and natural appearance, that they may detect change and prepare to meet the enemy half way; and the following remarks by Mr. Youatt are … plain and to the point, and I will … of such practical use to … when … and apply them, that I give them … : "It is the custom of … every horseman, who takes pains to … in the state of his patient, to turn down the lower eyelid, and to form his opinion of the degree of general inflammation by the colour which the lining membrane of … presents. If it is very red, he concludes that there is considerable fever; if it is of a pale pinkish hue, there is comparatively little danger. This is a very important examination, and the conclusion he draws from it is … true; but on the septum of the nose he has a membrane … continuous with those of the respiratory organs, … presenting a large surface, the ramifications of the blood … , and, what is truly important, indicating not only the … of the membranes, but of those with which it is … . We portion of the membrane which covers the lower part of the membrane of the nose—that which you can most readily bring into view—day after day, and under all the varying circumstances of health and disease; study it until you are enabled to recognise, and you soon will, and that with a degree of exactitude you would have scarcely thought possible, the pale pink hue when the horse is in health, the increasing blush of red and the general and uniform painting of the membrane betokening some excitement of the system—the streaked appearance when inflammation is threatening or commencing, the intensely florid red of inflammation becoming acute; the starting of the vessels from their gossamer coat and then seeming to run bare over the membrane when the inflammation is at the highest; the pale ground with patches of livid red, showing the half subdued but still existing fever; the uniform colour, but somewhat redder than natural, indicating a return to a healthy state of the circulation; the paleness approaching to white accompanying a state of debility, and yet some radiations of crimson showing that there is still considerable irritability, and that mischief may be in the wind; the pale livid colour warning you that the disease is assuming a typhoid character; the darker livid announcing that typhus is established, and that the vital current is stagnating; and the browner, dirty painting, intermingling with and subduing the lividness, and indicating that the game is up. These will be guides to our opinion and treatment which we can never too highly value." Catarrh having a tendency to extend and induce fever, with cough, sore throat, loss of appetite—for the horse will not eat if it pains him to swallow—and inflammation, it is most important to watch and check it in its earliest stages, when it is easily managed. The first symptom generally observed is a slight running at the nose, with sometimes a slighter weeping from the eyes, a little increased labour in breathing, caused by the passages being diminished by the thickening of the membrane, and also by their increased irritability. The producing causes are neglect of grooming, change of clothing, &c., and the treatment consists in removal of cause—placing the horse in a properly ventilated stable, where he can breathe cool, pure air, and have warm bedding and clothing. Give warm mashes, and what ostlers rather inconsistently term chilled water, meaning water with the chill taken off; and give in the mash six drachms to an ounce of powdered nitre. If the bowels are not affected by the mashes and soft food, it may be well to use an enema with that object; if it be accompanied by a swelling under the jaws, use a stimulating liniment, such as hartshorn and oil, with turpentine. To promote the discharge steaming is of great value. A hair bag, such as is used in making cider, should be a quarter filled with chaff, and boiling water poured over it, the steam being kept up by adding boiling water at intervals through a hole in the side of the bag, having a flap over it to prevent escape of steam.

Cold.—See *Catarrh.*

Colic.—Colic is of two kinds—spasmodic and windy colic, and the disease is known by other names, as gripes, fret, cramp, gullion, and belly ache, and, under one name or another, is well known to all who have had much to do with horses. Some horses are much more disposed to it than others, but all are liable to it under certain conditions, which are for the most part avoidable. The attacks of colic are always sudden, and of course unexpected, and often create unnecessary excitement and alarm, a state of things which is apt to lead to what is most to be avoided by permitting professedly knowing, but really ignorant persons, to adopt means for the animal's relief of such a nature as to run great risk of turning a comparatively harmless attack of colic into dangerous inflammation of the bowels. The causes generally producing colic are, giving of cold water to drink whilst the beast is warm, perhaps covered with sweat; or being exposed to cold when in that state will sometimes do it; the over eating of green food, or other food that the stomach fails thoroughly to digest; costiveness, too, is a not uncommon cause. Sometimes the administration of aloes is at the bottom of it, and it sometimes comes on unaccountably after a sharp drive. One of the surest symptoms by which to distinguish it is the sudden nature of its attack. The horse may be just taken out of the shafts, apparently quite well, and led into his stall, begin to eat, when all at once he stops, shakes himself, paws the litter with his fore feet, or stamps violently and looks round wistfully towards his flanks. The pain being severe he will kick at and even strike his belly with his hind feet. In some cases staling is profuse, in others he makes various attempts to void urine unsuccessfully. As the spasm passes he becomes quiet, and, with the absence of pain, returns to his manger and again begins to eat; shortly, however, the paroxysm of pain returns, and the horse shows uneasiness, shifting from side to side, pawing and kicking as before, showing a disposition to lie down, on doing which he will frequently roll on his back, kicking impatiently and evincing great pain, so intense indeed as frequently to cause him to sweat profusely.

The most important thing in such cases is for the stableman and horse owner to be able to distinguish clearly and confidently between colic and inflammation of the bowels, and the following are in substance the rules for so doing laid down by all recent veterinary authorities: In colic the attack is always sudden, in inflammation of the bowels the disease is gradual in its approach, marked by loss of appetite, uneasiness, fits of shivering, &c. In the first the pulse is not affected, except during the attacks of pain, when it is accelerated. In the second the pulse is considerably quickened, but small, not full, and difficult to feel. In the first relief is given by rubbing the belly. In the latter the belly is very tender, and gives pain on being touched; in the first motion gives ease, and a moderate trot or sharp walk will often give great relief, whereas in the latter the animal is not only averse to motion, but it evidently gives increased pain—in the former too—and this is a very marked distinction —the pain is intermittent, and when free from the paroxysms the horse seems right enough, but in inflammation the pain is constant. In the former the ears, legs, &c., are of their natural temperature; in the latter they are cold. In colic the strength of the horse is very little affected, whilst inflammation of the bowels produces rapid and great weakness.

Having determined that the attack is colic and not enteritis, as inflammation of the bowels is called, care must be taken that the treatment adopted and the supposed remedies given, are not of such a nature as to induce inflammation to take the place of the less dangerous disease. There is generally someone present on such occasions ready with advice gratis that had better be declined—harsh and violent means of cure never do any good, and are correspondingly dangerous; therefore, if anyone proposes a hard gallop, rubbing the belly with the tail of a stable broom, or violently kneading the belly with the knees, or proposing to place cayenne pepper, ginger, onions, &c., up the sheath, under the ignorant assumption that the horse merely wants to stale to be relieved, do not listen to him; gentleness in treating the horse is an important element of success in disease as in health, and to put the animal to additional and unnecessary pain is to cause him to knock about with every probability of producing the most serious results. Approach him quietly, and with coarse woollen cloths or hard wisps let a man on each side rub the belly continuously, or, if it can be done conveniently, apply a woollen rug, dipped in hot water, to the belly, covering it with a dry one and changing it as it gets cold. Gentle exercise, as before stated, will sometimes give relief, but it must not be more than a sharp walk or moderate trot. If it is suspected or known to have been brought on by costiveness, back raking should be resorted to, and injections of soap and warm water used to relieve the bowels, to which may be added a solution of aloes—about half-a-pint of decoction.

Of internal remedies, large and excessive doses of cayenne pepper, ginger, &c., and more especially large quantities of alcoholic spirits, whether alone or with the former, are dangerous, although, in moderate doses, they sometimes give relief, and are at times the only remedies at hand. Oil of turpentine in doses of from three to six ounces is a good anti-spasmodic in such cases, and is a favourite remedy, but care must be used in administering it, as if spilt over the animal it creates considerable irritation; it may be given floating on water or combined with linseed oil, or shaken into an emulsion with yolk of eggs or mucilage of gum arabic; it should, however, be given in connection with opium. Sulphuric ether is also a useful drug in colic—it is a diffusive stimulant—its action passes off quickly, and where relief is not obtained by the first dose it may be repeated in half-an-hour. Pimento has also been much extolled as an anti-spasmodic in these cases; it is given in form of a tincture made by macerating one pound of berries bruised in six pints of proof spirit for fourteen days, and then filtering, the dose being 3oz. to 4oz. The recipes for colic are innumerable, nearly every stableman having his own infallible cure; whilst the "gripe tinctures" of the druggists are countless. Turpentine has the advantage of being generally obtainable, and

4oz. of it in half a pint of linseed oil, with 2oz. of laudanum, will be found an excellent remedy. But one of the following preparations should be kept in readiness in every well regulated stable:

Colic, Feet, or Gripe Mixture.—Take sulphuric ether, 4 z.; laudanum, 8oz.; mix and keep in a well stoppered bottle, in a cool place. Dose, 2oz. to 3oz, given in solution of aloes, or in gruel, or sound ale; repeated, if necessary, in half an hour, the aloes being omitted from the second dose.

The following is the gripe tincture or preparation for spasmodic colic of "The Field Horse Medicine Chest," and will be found a valuable remedy, it should be kept at hand, as it does not deteriorate with age.

Gripe Tincture.—Take tincture of opium made with spirit of nitrous ether, instead of proof spirit, 8oz.; tincture of pimento, as ordered to be prepared above, 1oz.; sulphuric ether, 4oz.; mix, keep in a glass stoppered bottle in a cool place. Dose, 2oz. or 3oz. to be given as ordered for other remedies.

Windy or flatulent colic differs from the spasmodic, it is caused by indigestion; the food fermenting in the stomach and bowels, distending the latter with the gas thus generated, the belly is blown out like a cow suffering from hoven, and the horse is in considerable pain; old horses are most subject to it. The following will be found a useful remedy for it:

Flatulence Mixture.—Aromatic spirit of ammonia, 1½oz.; laudanum, 1½oz.; tincture of capsicum, 1dr.; bicarbonate of soda, 1oz.; in 1½pts. of hot ale.

The solutions of chlorinated soda and lime are also prescribed in these cases.

After a horse has suffered from an attack of colic he should receive extra care and attention for some time; the stable should be warm and well ventilated; the dry food should be partially withheld, and steamed corn and mashes substituted, or bruised oats with a mash, and a few carrots and green food, but given sparingly; the water should also have the chill taken off it, especially in cold weather; in fact, the horse's comfort should, under such circumstances, be studied with more than ordinary care, and to aid his digestion he might be indulged with a sprinkling of good condiment over his food, a recipe for which will be given further on.

Constipation.—See *Costiveness*.

Contusions.—See *Bruises*.

Corns.—Corns on the human foot are pretty generally known to most people, being one of the unpleasant and unwelcome attendants on civilisation, for they arise in fashionable boots and shoes. But with corns in the foot of the horse, they are rarely if ever seen in the unshod colt or filly—being the result of unnatural pressure as in the human foot. This, however, is the only resemblance. The corn in the foot of the horse has a red spongy appearance, and is very sensitive and tender to pressure, and generally confined to the fore feet, which endure more pressure—the seat being generally at the inner angle of the sole between the crust and the bars. Two classes of feet are particularly liable to corns; the contracted foot (too often the result of a fanciful system of shoeing that pays no attention to the nature and structure of the foot it attempts to improve), for in this the thick hard sole does not yield to the motion of the other parts, and the sensitive sole gets injured by the pressure, and then inflammation is the result. The flat fleshy foot with low weak heels is the most subject to corns, because, in this case, the sensitive sole is not protected by firm hoof, and being placed low when the coffin bone descends, it gets squeezed and injured between that and the shoe; for these reasons a horse with high heels should have his foot well pared at each time of shoeing, whereas the horse with weak thin heels should, especially on the inner heel, be spared the knife. Corns are caused by wearing the shoe too long without changing it, also by gravel getting into the foot, and also getting placed under a partially loose shoe and causing irregularity of tread, and consequent uneven pressure, and also from many forms of bad shoeing. Corns are apt to be treated rather too lightly, but when neglected the inflammation goes on to suppuration, and that neglected may produce quittor. In searching for corns it is usual for the farriers to do so by pressure with the the pincers round the foot; of course pressure over a tender, inflamed part like a corn will cause the horse to flinch, and although some horses, more sensitive than others will yield and flinch under the pressure even when a corn does not exist, it is still a pretty correct way of judging where the corn is if the lameness arises from that cause. The angle between the crust and the bars should be well pared out, almost to the quick, but not so as to injure the sensitive sole. If there is no discharge of matter, or none formed, the place may be lightly touched over with butyr of antimony, and then a shoe contrived so as to relieve the part from pressure; if the smith is too stupid, or what is more likely to be the case, obstinate over some pig-headed notion of his own, the horse owner should see the work done himself. If suppuration has taken place, the paring must extend right to the bottom of the corn, so as to let out the matter, and all loose pieces of horn separated or separating from the rest should be cut away. The foot should then be either placed in warm water or poultices applied to clear the matter out, and reduce the inflammation.

The prevention of corns is best accomplished by an intelligent study of the peculiarities of the horse's foot, and the adoption of a style of shoeing in accordance with it. This is to the interest as it is the duty of every horse owner, and many slight modifications of the greatest practical good will suggest themselves to observant persons. The shoe should be made to fit the foot, not the foot to fit the shoe, as is too often the case.

Costiveness or Constipation.—By this is understood that the discharge of fæces is irregular, at long intervals, or altogether stopped, and the dung when voided is hard and dry, sometimes covered with a glairy matter. This state of things is oftener a symptom of disease than existing as a disease in itself, and is a sign that should never be overlooked, or its early warning neglected. It is often a symptom of jaundice; it produces colic; and there is always a danger of inflammation of the bowels following when it is not early attended to. Some horses are naturally of a costive habit, and require to be dieted with additional care in consequence, as whenever confined to heating and stimulating food, such as corn and beans, constipation takes place, but with all such horses the evil is easily prevented and the tendency corrected by an occasional mash in lieu of corn, a daily allowance of green food in the season, and at other times a portion of carrots or other roots chopped up carefully, and mixed with the chaff and corn. When the costiveness does not at once yield to the dieting alone, no time should be lost in resorting to additional means to procure the desired result, most important of which will be backraking, and the injection of clysters of warm gruel with castor oil, or a solution of aloes may be added, or about ½lb. of Epsom salts dissolved in every gallon, or soap and water lukewarm may be used with 1oz. of spirit of turpentine to each quart and thoroughly mixed by agitation before being injected, or a solution of common salt may be tried instead of either of the above; the backraking, however, must precede the use of the clysters, as otherwise the hardened fæces would effectually prevent the admission of the liquid. In backraking, the hand, by placing the thumb and fingers close together lengthwise, will be cone shaped, and, after dipping in olive oil or otherwise well greasing it, it is introduced into the rectum, and all the hardened fæces removed. This must be done more than once before the enemas are used, and it should be undertaken by a person with a small hand; this is a very needful operation which any groom may do with care, and it should always be resorted to in cases where it is found necessary to give a horse physic without having been previously prepared with mashes, &c. I may here observe that it is a dangerous practice to give purgatives in case of costiveness before back-raking and enemas have been used, and that in using the latter a small quantity is likely to have no effect, and that from one to two gallons at last should be thrown up. If during the existence of costiveness the pulse is found to quicken much, and the belly become tender to the touch, the horse may be bled. Prevention of costiveness and its results will be achieved by correct dieting and watchfulness over the horse's general health.

Cough.—We are all too familiar with coughs, both in ourselves and our domestic animals, all of which, in common with us, are subject to it. Cough is an effort of the lungs to get rid of extraneous and irritating matter. The muscles of the respiratory organs are set in motion, and by a sudden spasmodic action the air from the lungs and passages leading to them is violently expelled, carrying with it phlegm and other matter that may have collected, and that interferes with the free passage of the air. Cough is symptomatic of disease, not a disease in itself; and of the many varieties of cough which we recognise, each has its peculiarity, which to the experienced and attentive gives pretty sure indication of the seat of the disease. Cough is produced by worms in the intestines, in which cases the lungs act sympathetically with the irritation caused by these parasites; if worms be the cause, a variable appetite, and a harsh, dirty staring coat will also exist as additional symptoms, and then, after one or two mashes, the following vermifuge might with advantage be given as a drench:

Vermifuge.—2oz. of spirit of turpentine, 1oz. of laudanum, 1½ pints of linseed oil; this should be followed by linseed tea or oatmeal gruel. Cough is also a symptom of various diseases of the lungs and air passages from the slight irritation that exists often in the lining membrane of the outer passages, to bronchitis and inflammation of the lungs; it accompanies thick and broken wind, is caused by glanders—a disease seated near to and affecting the air passages—and is also often present in diseases of the stomach and bowels.

Some of these diseases on their disappearance leave behind them such an over-sensitiveness and irritability of the air-pipes, that the horse is ever after liable to a cough more or less severe, which is brought on with any change of temperature, as being taken from the stable to the outer air, changing from a warm stable to a colder one, or *vice versâ*, and frequently after drinking.

Although a horse with one of those irritating chronic coughs may go on for years doing useful work, he is predisposed to the more dangerous forms of disease of the respiratory organs, and must on that account receive special care, and be closely watched, and any increase in the severity of the affection should not pass unheeded; much may be done to alleviate suffering and prevent serious consequences by a wise and prudent attention to the proper feeding of the horse and his comfort in the stable. An ill-ventilated, close, filthy stable is in itself sufficient to set up a cough; and an animal whose wind pipes are exceptionally sensitive should not have dry food and chaff. Dusty hay should be carefully avoided, and all corn and cut hay or straw should be damped; and in cases where the stomach is involved, the use of green food or roots in addition will be an advantage. When the cough is unusually severe the following ball may be occasionally given, but not too often, as the medicines are powerful and not to be made too free with.

Cough Ball.—Powdered digitalis 20 grains, tartar emetic ½ drachm, nitre 2 d…, hips, tar ½oz., linseed meal to form a ball.

An old-fashioned demulcent medicine of great use in allaying the irritability in these cases is the marsh mallow, and benefit will often be found to arise from giving it with linseed in a mash two or three times a week.

Marsh Mallow Demulcent.—Take 4oz. or 8oz. of the root, according as it is dry or fresh, and boil it well over a slow fire in a gallon of water, and take the root out by straining, and, adding more water, boil in it half a pint of linseed, and mix the lot in a bran mash.

If the cough is supposed to be connected with disordered stomach, it will be removed by attention to diet, giving a dose of physic and a few cordial balls, such as the following:

Cordial Balls.—Ground ginger ½oz., carraways 2dr., gentian 2dr., oil of pimento 15 drops, treacle to form a ball.

Cracked Heels.—Cracked heels occur from several causes, and white-legged horses, and those with fleshy legs are most liable to it. The skin there secretes a kind of greasy matter, which keeps it soft and pliable, and assists in throwing off wet; the hair, too, when left on, helps to prevent grit and dirt reaching the skin, and exercising an irritating effect on it. As wet and dirt are an active cause in producing cracked heels, we, of course, most often find the horse suffering in this way in wet dirty weather; the skin, by the constant action of wet and cold, gets dried, stretches and cracks, and from the cracks there is discharged a watery matter. Previous to this there is heat and itching of the part, and the horse may be seen rubbing one foot against the other, the heels of the hind feet being most affected. Dirty stables are also a cause of cracked heels, as they are of so many other ills. A horse kept standing, with his heels exposed to the noxious exhalations from accumulated dung and urine is sure to feel the irritating effects of the acrid gases these matters are constantly giving out. Horses turned out to winter, especially on low ground, often suffer severely, the skin sloughing and ulcerating; sometimes the skin is considerably thickened, with deep fissures which discharge serous matter. When the ulceration is superficial, only skin deep, simple remedies will put matters to rights. Poultices of bran, linseed meal, or of turnips or carrots, boiled till quite soft and then beaten into a pulp, will be almost a cure in themselves; if anything else is needed, an astringent lotion applied two or three times a day and the heels rubbed with glycerine before applying the poultice will be found beneficial.

Astringent Lotion.—Sulphate of zinc, 3 drachms to a pint of water, or a decoction of oak bark, made by boiling 2oz. in a quart of water down to a pint.

Where the sores are deeper and sloughing, they should be—after sponging any matter out—touched with butyr of antimony or a solution of caustic, 1 scruple of nitrate of silver to an ounce of water, and a lotion of the permanganate of potash (Condy's Fluid), may be used.

In some cases it may be necessary to give a dose of physic and a course of cooling and alterative medicine.

As means of prevention attention should be paid to cleanliness in the stable, and very particular attention paid to the thorough drying of the parts when washed; if the heels are left wet by the groom the evaporation that goes on in the stable robs them of their natural heat, and they get dry and cracked, so that when a horse's legs are washed, they should be rubbed until thoroughly dry, indeed until they glow with heat, and when this cannot be insured it is better to leave the legs unwashed and let the rough of the dirt be brushed off, and when quite dry the remainder brushed out. As cracked heels are supposed to be in some cases caused by want of vitality, or brisk circulation, the groom cannot, therefore, give them too much friction, and in cases where horses are predisposed to it, I would recommend after washing and drying, to rub a little of this liniment over the heels.

Liniment for Cracked Heels.—Spirits of wine ½oz., Goulard's extract 1oz., olive oil 6½oz.

Arsenic is given as an alterative in obstinate cases, from its action on the skin, but its use is best left to the professional man.

Cramp.—See *Colic.*

Crib-biting.—There are few more undesirable animals to possess than a crib-biter. Not only is the habit a most unpleasant one to witness, but as a rule it renders the horse incapable of doing his work, at least with that dash and energy that is so pleasing, and they generally present a lean and lank appearance most annoying to a man who takes a pride in his cattle, and who knows that his liberal system of feeding and general care should produce a more creditable result. Crib-biters are also more subject to colic than others, and as some hold that the habit is contracted by imitatation they are not desirable inmates of a stable. The general opinion leans to crib-biting as being a result of some derangement of the digestive organs, and that may be brought about in many ways, through unhealthy stables, bad keep, musty oats or hay, &c., but it also comes on horses well fed, and more particularly those kept too much to sameness of food, and too closely confined to the stable. Youatt suggests as an occasional cause the groom dressing the horse in the stable where he can get hold of the manger with his teeth. The habit is too well known to need much description—the "cribber" lays hold of the edge of the manger or any other convenient place, and, stretching out his neck with a convulsive action, seems to belch out a little wind with an unpleasant grunt, he will then gulp down air till his belly swells and till, in some instances, he is evidently in pain, and, pawing and striking with his fore feet, lies down and rolls as in gripes.

The effect of cribbing is sometimes to break, always to wear the teeth; crib-biting is often done when feeding and with the mouth full, so that it causes great waste of corn, and as much saliva in this way escapes, digestion is interfered with by the loss of it, and by the imperfect mastication through broken or worn teeth, it keeps up the indigestion which may have been its own original cause. The most effectual treatment for a crib biter is to render the habit impossible by putting him under the restraint of a bar muzzle, which is so made as to enable the horse to reach his hay, &c., with his lips and tongue, but not to take hold of any object such as the edge of the manger, with his teeth. A simpler and much cheaper appliance is the strap round the throat; but to be effectual it must be worn so tight as to run the risk of setting up local inflammation, and thus create a greater evil than it is designed to cure.

Tonics given regularly as an aid to digestion will prove beneficial, and Mayhew recommends a lump of rock salt in the manger, and the corn and cut stuff to be sprinkled with magnesia. If the digestive powers are carefully strengthened, and the horse is caused to wear the muzzle a sufficient length of time, he may forget the bad habit, but a crib-biter is a horse to be carefully avoided in adding to our equine stock. In law it constitutes unsoundness.

Curb.—A curb is a hard callous swelling on the hind part of the hock, and some inches below its point. A horse throws out a curb suddenly on being quickly pulled up in a fast gallop, or on taking an extra leap, especially on hard unyielding ground. Tendency to curb is hereditary, and it is therefore not desirable to breed from horse or mare with it the progeny being specially liable to throw them out when called on for rapid exertion. Such horses as are cow-hocked—that is, with the hocks leaning in towards each other, and the legs as a consequence, bent out at an angle, as is peculiar to cows,—are very liable to have curbs, as the formation causes a greater strain on the tendons of these parts.

The cause is a sprain of the sheath of the tendons or of the ring-like ligament that binds them, and, of course, there is at first inflammation, so that the first thing to be done is to reduce that by the application of poultices, or of the cooling lotions (p. 9) such as has been prescribed in other cases of local inflammation. A lotion composed as under will answer.

Cooling Lotion.—Equal parts of spirits of wine and strong vinegar to three parts of cold water.

It will also be necessary to attend to the diet, giving mashes, green food, and, when sufficiently prepared for it, a dose of physic should be given. It is also sometimes necessary to bleed from the thigh vein, but that only when it is seen that the other means are ineffectual in reducing the inflammation. When this has been successfully accomplished, a blister should be applied, and the red iodide of mercury (p. 24) is the best for preventing the formation of the hard and callous substance, or of dispersing it if it has commenced to form; the way to apply this has already been explained. As the parts are always left much weakened, the horse should have long rest, and be very gradually brought back to his work; but the sinews will be much strengthened if, when the blister has healed and during the time of rest, liberal application is made, with plenty of friction, of a good stimulating liniment.

D.

Diabetes or Profuse Staling.—Diabetes is a disease to which the horse is rarely subject, at least in its worst form, such as corresponds to the *diabetes mellitus* of the human subject, although an immoderate flow of urine is not so uncommon in stables where diuretics are too often and injudiciously used; for it is a very common superstition that when anything ails the horse, no matter what, he must be made to stale, and hence medicines having this effect are too often resorted to and given in overdoses, such as to produce profuse staling, and sometimes this becomes true diabetes. Food of bad quality is said to cause diabetes, and mow-burnt hay and new oats are said to have a special tendency to produce it; it is always accompanied by very great thirst, and quickly weakens and emaciates the animal. The horse suffering from this disease is not likely to be cured, but it may be alleviated by attention to his general comfort, and a fair allowance of green food and roots, especially of carrots, will be beneficial. The leaves of the bear-berry or bear's whortleberry (*uva ursi*) is recommended for it, and the following ball might be tried, giving one every day.

Ball for Diabetes.—Take dried leaves of *uva ursi* in powder half an ounce, opium in powder ½dr., gallic acid ½dr., common mass sufficient to form a ball. Mayhew recommends 1dr. of iodide of iron, to be given in form of a ball daily, or 1oz. of diluted phosphoric acid in a pint of water night and morning.

Diarrhœa or Excessive Purging.—This is also called looseness, scouring, &c., &c., and is often a simple effort of nature to relieve the bowels from some obnoxious and irritating substance, as partially digested food; it is often set up by over doses of physic, and among the numerous causes a too sudden change of diet, especially from dry corn and hay to a superabundance of green and succulent grasses, giving water immediately before driving sharply, a sudden chill, or even a change to water different to that which the animal has been accustomed to. Those horses not well ribbed up, called "washy," are held to be most subject to it; and whenever a horse is known to be so he should be the more carefully dieted and given drier and more binding food. In diarrhœa avoid medicine if possible, in most cases it will not be required. Keep the horse quiet and warm, clothing both body and legs; do not, however, keep the animal in a close stuffy place, but where there is free ventilation and the air kept at a pretty regular temperature; remove all corn and hay, also green food, and give oatmeal gruel, rice boiled soft, gruel of wheaten flour, boiled linseed, and other demulcents that will be easily digested and be soothing to the animal; if this treatment alone fails, the following injection may be used.

Injection for Diarrhœa.—Boiled starch made thin, and with an ounce of laudanum to each quart; or, if not found effectual, use gruel a quart, laudanum 1½oz., and tincture of catechu 1oz.

It must be borne in mind that it is not desirable to check diarrhœa too suddenly, but better to clear the bowels of any irritant by means of the gruel, &c., when it will generally subside without further interference on our part, but it is always necessary not to go back too suddenly to the ordinary food for fear of causing a relapse. In diarrhœa the patient is sometimes relieved by rubbing the belly with a strong stimulating liniment, or applying hot clothes frequently changed. When medicine has to be resorted to, the best thing is chalk with opium and catechu. The following may be given in severe and obstinate cases:

Drench for Diarrhœa.—Prepared chalk, 2oz.; extract of catechu, 1dr.; powdered gum acacia, 1½oz.; laudanum, 1oz.; aromatic spirit of ammonia, ½oz.; water sufficient to make one and a half pints to be given as a drench every six hours.

Dysentery.—This is a disease very uncommon in the horse; it is marked by dark coloured, very offensive discharges, consisting of hard lumps of fæces covered with mucous, mixed with fluid of a purulent nature, sometimes tinged with blood. It was formerly, and still is in some districts, as are also bad cases of simple diarrhœa, called "*molten grease*," from a belief that it was the fat of the body dissolved and discharged by the bowels. Bartlett, a writer on horse diseases, thus speaks of it: "By molten grease is meant a fatty or oily discharge with the dung, and it arises from a colliquation or melting down of the fat of a horse's body by violent exercise in very hot weather." I need scarcely say that this untenable idea has long since been banished to the dark corners of the land; but incredible as it may appear, I have heard the absurdity stoutly upheld by men who were entrusted with the treatment of thousands of pounds' worth of valuable stock—entrusted, too, by men of intelligence and shrewdness in most matters, but who persist in making a mystery of medicine and believing in the empyric rather than the educated veterinarian. The causes of dysentery are chiefly bad food, grazing on the poor washy herbage of low marshy ground, and neglected cases of diarrhœa. The greater attention that is now paid to the proper feeding and general sanitary condition of horses, helped by the advance in their medical treatment —although this latter has been comparatively slight, thanks to the obstinacy of horse owners—cases of dysentery, as before said, are now rare. When they do occur, the general directions for diarrhœa should be followed; and it will be a wise policy to at once consult a qualified veterinary surgeon, who, even if he fails to save the horse, will, by pointing out errors in early treatment and probable causes giving rise to the disease, have given good exchange for his fee, as will be fully proved if his advice be taken for future guidance. Neither diarrhœa nor dysentery are infectious, although the former may exist as an epidemic.

E.

Enteritis — Inflammation of the Bowels.—This is a very dangerous disease, and all the more so as it is often confounded with that known by the various names of colic, fret, gripes, and belly-ache, &c., and which has been already treated under colic where the most clearly distinguishing features have been given—both diseases are marked by considerable pain, and the horse shows it in both cases by pawing the ground, striking at the belly, and looking round dolorously towards the flank. In colic the pain is intermittent, whereas in enteritis it is constant, although sometimes accompanied with spasm and paroxysms of greater pain, when the horse will crouch with his belly to the ground, or lie down, roll over, and kick, and getting up again pant with pain, whilst the sweat rolls off him.

Inflammation comes on more gradually than colic, which is always sudden in its appearance, and is marked by loss of appetite, feverishness, and general depression, and dulness. The pulse is always increased, but is small and wiry, and the ears and extremities are cold; the animal will sometimes be alternately covered with sweat, and suffering cold tremors, none of which symptoms indicate colic; the mouth and tongue are also very hot and dry, a certain indication of inflammation. In this disease the horse loses strength rapidly, pressure on the belly causes pain, as does any quicker motion than a quiet walk, whereas, in colic, the animal retains his strength, is often eased by a moderate trot, and rubbing the belly gives relief.

Inflammation of the bowels sometimes follows castration; it is often caused by giving powerful medicines injudiciously, as for instance strong physic balls without proper preparation, or it may be induced by improper food, causing constipation; and it not unfrequently is the result of neglected or improperly treated colic; so that horse owners should be careful to use only approved remedies and means of relief in that comparatively simple and innocent disease, and avoid the rough measures and stupid nostrums so much in vogue.

By way of treatment the first thing to be done is to bleed freely from the jugular vein, taking away blood quickly in a full stream, and almost to fainting. The bowels must be relieved, and to accomplish this both backraking (p. 30), as already explained, and a very free use of clysters, should be resorted to, and purgatives should be also given.

Drench for Enteritis.—Some veterinarians give linseed oil; Walsh prescribes a pint with 2oz. of laudanum, every six hours, till the bowels are relieved; whilst Percival depends on aloes, and prescribes it in the following form: compound decoction of aloes, 4oz.; spirit of sulphuric ether and laudanum, each 2oz.; warm water, a pint; given as a drench, and repeated each two hours with only half the quantity of aloes, till four doses are given.

Compound Decoction of Aloes.—The form Percival gives for the compound decoction of aloes is as follows: take Barbadoes aloes, 2oz.; bicarbonate of potash, 2oz.; gum acacia, 2oz.; water, 1 pint; dissolve gently with heat, and add, when cold, sufficient spirit of wine to keep it. The product should be 1 pint and a quarter.

By way of external application hot fomentations should be constantly used, or a cantharidine blister—a liquid one, either made with vinegar or turpentine—applied, or a poultice of strong mustard and vinegar well rubbed in.

In cases like inflammation of the bowels, which is so dangerous and rapid in its progress, the aid of the veterinary surgeon should be early sought; but if unattainable, the above will be the best treatment to adopt.

F.

False Quarter.—False quarter is absence of a portion of the hard or outer horn, caused by the destruction of or injury to a part of the coronary substance which secretes the horn. It presents a gap or groove running down from the coronet, which is only covered with a layer of soft horn insufficient to protect the sensitive parts thus deprived of their natural strong hard covering, and rendering the foot liable to severe accident, from the jarring caused by the horse in travelling; and dirt getting into the exposed spongy horn, irritation is set up, when it may crack, and bleeding and discharge of matter follow. In this case the fleshy part protrudes in form of fungoid granulations, and is apt to get pressed between the edges of the separated hard horn, and in such case further inflammation is excited and lameness ensues; this state of the case calls for rest, with fomentations, poultices, and other means for reducing local inflammations. False quarter is more the consequence of other diseases, as quittor, canker, &c., having destroyed the power of the coronary substance to secrete horn, than a disease in itself; but it is also caused by the horse treading on the coronet, or from external injury from some other cause, as the tread of another horse, a kick or bruise; it renders the horse liable to lameness and greatly weakens that side of the hoof. The peculiar function of the coronary substance to deposit horn being destroyed, art cannot restore it; and, therefore, treatment of its result—the partial absence of outer hard horn, forming the groove called false quarter—is necessarily palliative only. It is necessary, as far as possible, to relieve the weakened quarter from pressure, and this can be done in the case of a strong foot by paring and levelling off the horn on each side of the groove, so that direct contact and pressure of the shoe may be avoided. This cannot be done with a horse having a thin hoof; but the bar shoe, which in such cases is needed, should have an indentation corresponding to the diseased part, which will answer the same end. The fissure itself should be kept filled with the hoof ointment prescribed for brittle hoof (p. 15), pouring it on when slightly melted, when it will harden and protect the part. This will require frequent renewal, and it must not be done while there is any tenderness, bleeding, or discharge, which, as before said, must be treated as other local inflammations and sores, by poultices, &c., and a dressing of nitric acid lotion, carbolic acid lotion (p. 17), or powered blue stone if required.

Nitric Acid Lotion.—Pure nitric acid 2dr.; water half pint.

The bar shoe being worn, a horse with false quarter may be used, as he will travel very well, and it is only when there is lameness from the soft exposed parts being injured that absolute rest is required. To restore the coronary ligament which has been divided by cut, bruise, or other cause, to its natural state and enable it to renew its function of secreting horn, blistering the coronet, or the application of a suitable heated iron, is advised by some writers, but success is at least doubtful. When attempted, every help should be given, by rest, thinning the edge of the horn at either side of the crack, supporting the hoof as far as possible, drawing the separated parts together, by a plaster of pitch, &c. If the blister is tried, it will require repetition after the first is quite healed. The first symptoms of success will be seen in the growth of new united horn from the coronet towards the sole.

Farcy and Glanders.—These are the most insidious, dangerous, and malignant diseases to which our horses are subject, lying in ambush behind the simulations of less harmful and more tractable ills. The unwary and inexperienced owner, whose wish is often father to the thought that the fell destroyer—that has baffled veterinary science from the days of Hippocrates to the present—is merely his more ordinary acquaintances surfeit or common cold, is thereby induced to become a powerful auxiliary force in spreading the dread contagion, and in the destruction of his own stock, at the same time running the terrible risk of himself, servants, or friends becoming the victims of the horrible disease he is unwittingly fostering, which, once contracted, is almost sure to end in the most painful death. So dreadfully dangerous is it recognised to be, and its incurable nature, in the present state of veterinary science, so completely accepted, that a special Act of Parliament exists to secure its limitation to those known to be actually diseased, by making compulsory their isolation and destruction, and the cleansing and disinfection of stables and fittings, &c., where such diseased animals have been; neglect of which course is visited with pains and penalties, as described in the Contagious Diseases (Animals) Act.

Farcy and glanders are so intimately connected that they are considered one and the same disease in different forms or stages; in fatal cases of the former glanders always makes a prominent appearance before death, and the peculiar forms assumed in farcy—the "buttons" and larger lumps which indicate it—being the result of the action of a virus on the absorbent vessels, it would appear that the poison of glanders must be in the system before farcy makes itself apparent.

The first noticeable symptoms of farcy is the appearance of the small lumps, in size from a shilling to half-a-crown, known as farcy buds or buttons. These generally present themselves on the lips, neck, and inside the arms and thighs; and spreading, soon form a network of lumps or buttons, connected with hardened cord-like veins, which are the indurated or hardened lymphatic or absorbent vessels.

These lumps are at first hard, but become soft, and when they break or are opened, discharge at first a healthy matter, but this soon changes, becoming foul, offensive, and abhorrent. The ulcers formed are depressed in the centre with raised ragged edges of fungoid growth difficult to heal. It is a usual practice to burn them with the budding iron, and, after the slough caused by this has come off, to dress with a strong solution of corrosive sublimate or pure carbolic acid and glycerine, one part of the former to two of the latter. The buds or buttons are often subjected to the treatment of the iron before they break. In some few cases these farcy lumps become very hard, and remain so for many months, lulling the unsuspicious into a dangerous carelessness; but the evil, although dormant for the time, is sure sooner or later to break out with renewed force.

There is great danger of the ignorant and inexperienced mistaking farcy buttons for the lumps that appear in surfeit, but, in the latter, they spread over the body, and are never connected by the hardened cord-like vessels noticed as peculiarly indicative of farcy. The eruptions in surfeit are pustular, and do not end in unhealthy ulcers, but in desquamation, or peeling off of the cuticle.

In some cases the legs swell enormously; a hinder leg being generally attacked. The swelling takes place very suddenly, and the whole leg, from hock to thigh, may become three times its ordinary size. This is accompanied by feverishness; but these symptoms need not be mistaken for grease, with which they are apt to be confounded; for in grease there is not only redness of the skin, but it is stretched rigidly, and there is always scurf and cracks.

In other cases the muzzle swells considerably, and this is generally followed by a discharge of offensive matter from the nose. The horse becomes mangy and hide bound. Other general symptoms of farcy are the appetite failing or, on the other hand, being extremely voracious. Intense thirst is also generally present.

Before mentioning the causes giving rise to farcy, or the methods of cure adopted, it will be more convenient to refer to glanders.

Glanders, as already observed, is so very intimately connected with farcy that they cannot easily be separated, and are by many looked on as different stages and phases of the same disease. In the first stage of glanders there is a continuous discharge of thin, watery, transparent matter, from one or both nostrils, but generally from one only, and that in the vast majority of cases the left, a most singular fact, which has not been accounted for. This discharge is distinguished from that of common cold by its chronic character, as it may continue unchanged for many months without affecting the general health of the horse; yet in this stage the disease is infectious, showing what great care is necessary to distinguish it, and by isolation prevent the spread of so dire a malady. During this first stage the discharge is small and constant, and never sticky, and is free from smell. And if with these features the discharge is confined to one nostril, the disease is certainly glanders.

In the second stage the discharge considerably increases, becoming thicker and sticky, the glands under the jaw enlarge, and become attached to the bone. This cannot be mistaken for strangles, a disease incident to young horses, for in strangles it is not a single gland that is swollen, but the whole substance between the jaws; in strangles there is always cough, the discharge from the nose is thick from the beginning, and the lining membrane of the nostrils has the redness of inflammation, whereas in glanders that member has neither that vivid red appearance nor the pale pink of health, but is of a leaden or purple hue, or some shade between, and this is in itself an important feature symptomatic of glanders.

As the disease runs on sores of a chancrous character appear inside the nostrils; these are deep and ulcerous, with sunken centres and raised ragged edges, and are connected by varicose veins, these in some cases extending to the larynx, causing difficulty of breathing. There is general constitutional disturbance, the appetite fails, flesh is rapidly lost, the horse is spiritless, legs swell in the day, going down at night, coat staring, harsh, and unthrifty, and readily comes off, ulcerous sores break out on the body, and the horse, exhausted, dies. From what has been said it should appear that glanders need not be mistaken for any other disease, if due attention be paid to symptoms. Horse owners should specially beware of all chronic discharges from the nostrils, especially in weak worn-out horses, for it is the old and the overworked that are the marks for this fell disease. If there is the smallest doubt as to the nature of the disease, it is an imperative duty to call in a qualified veterinarian to decide the question and advise as to treatment.

Whatever may be the cause of glanders, it is well known that too severe work with indifferent feeding pave the way for it. When the horse, exhausted, requires rest and quiet, with the natural stimulation afforded by warm mashes and easily digested food, has his flagged energies roused by the administration of strong stimulants and heating cordials, such as foolish grooms delight to resort to, a premium is offered for an attack of glanders.

Filthy and ill-ventilated stables are a fertile source of this, as of so many other diseases incidental to the horse; and if our very imperfect sanitary laws were carried out in the rural districts, glanders in the stable and fever in the cottage would both be less frequent; but as it is these laws are a sham, a wise Government having left their administration in the hands of the farmers, who are not only themselves the greatest offenders, but are, as a class, incapable of appreciating the great value of sanitary measures, and too penurious to spend money for results which they have not eyes to see.

In all cases prevention is better than cure, and in farcy and glanders it is the only thing, as no cure is known, although isolated cases of recovery from farcy are recorded. Blaine gives the case of a horse suffering from farcy being turned into a field of tares and let take his chance, and although the animal could not move about, he ate his way among the tares and ultimately recovered. The preventive measures are—keeping animals from contact with those diseased, and places where glandered horses have been; a precaution adopted by everyone to the best of their knowledge and power. Too great care cannot be used in this matter, considering how powerfully infectious the disease is, even in its most incipient stages. The stables at inns and public mews ought to be kept with care, and disinfectants used in them at regular intervals; not altogether as a prevention of this disease, but to render the place more sweet and wholesome, and prevent unseen and unsuspected accidents of this nature. A tendency to glanders is considered to be hereditary, therefore it behoves the breeder to use every care in the selection of mare and stallion, and to be assured as far as possible that neither come from a glandered stock.

As the disease is the special heritage of the poor over-worked brute, worn out in the hard service of another brute, who in return "stuffs his ribs with mouldy hay," self-interest joins humanity in the appeal that kind treatment and consideration for age and infirmities should be practised, and that the horse as well as the man deserves "a fair day's wage for a fair day's work."

The grossly filthy state in which some stables are kept, the manure being allowed to accumulate in dark corners, poisoning the little fresh air that finds its way into buildings built to prevent, not secure, ventilation, is a great encourager of glanders, as the horse that is compelled to breath vitiated air must soon lose in vital energy, and thus the seed-bed is prepared for the propagation of any disease-germs that may exist, if it does not, in fact, produce them.

Glanders rarely or never finds its way into the stables of gentlemen, and can only do so by unfortunate direct contagion, because the conditions that induce and foster that and other diseases are not allowed to exist. The stables are lofty, light, well ventilated, and kept thoroughly clean—conditions within the reach of all who keep a horse if they choose to adopt them.

As to treatment, although we would advise on the slightest suspicion of danger that a qualified veterinary surgeon be called in, we will briefly refer to one or two methods of treatment that have been adopted. There is an old and cruel practice among farriers and others of slitting open the horse's nostril and scraping the cartilage, searing the glands, and firing the frontal and nasal bones; others inject mixtures of strong mustard and capsicum, solutions of corrosive sublimate and vitriol, &c. This is needless cruelty, suggested by a short-sighted ignorance, and can only give the most excruciating pain without a reasonable hope of doing good, and, of course, should never be permitted. A much more sensible and more humane treatment was advised by that old writer Markham, which was to take the Auripigmentum (sulphuret of arsenic), or King's yellow, as it is called, Tussilago (colt's-foot), and crude imperitim, and having beaten them into a mass burn a part under a funnel placed on a dish or piece of hot sheet iron, and fumigate the horse.

The medicines that have been found of most use in farcy and those diseases that simulate glanders, and that would without attention in all probability degenerate into glanders, are the diniodide of copper, combined with cantharides and tonics. The following formula may be adopted:

Powders for Glanders.—Diniodide of copper, 6 dr.; powdered cantharides, ½ dr.; powdered gentian root, 4oz.; cayenne pepper, 2 scruples; very carefully mixed and divided into four equal doses, one to be given night and morning; and the treatment to be continued for some weeks.

The diniodide, like all the preparations of copper, acts as a tonic on the horse, but it also has a powerful influence on the absorbent vessels. It is a powerful remedy, and therefore must be used with considerable circumspection, and if it causes much soreness of the diseased part, and there is a failing appetite and general derangement, it should be withheld for a time and again resorted to. As before stated, however, in all cases, suspected or confirmed, the professional veterinary should be applied to at once where possible, on account of the insidious and dangerous character of the disease.

Fever in the Feet.—See *Foot Founder*.

Fistula.—A fistula is a deep narrow ulcer, callous or hardened, and generally arising from an abscess. Although the term might be as properly applied to poll evil, custom has, when the horse is the subject, generally confined it to that disease known as fistulous withers.

There is, however, fistula of the parotid duct, which is a sinuous opening into the duct which discharges the saliva, and which enlarges, and, becoming callous, allows the saliva to escape in large quantities. This is sometimes the result of abscess arising from strangles.

This is treated by setting up a degree of inflammation of the part, and closing the orifice with pledgets of cotton wool saturated with collodion, but the cure is best left to a practical hand.

Fistulous Withers.—The state of disease known as fistulous withers is now comparatively rare, and should never occur at all, as it is a preventable form of suffering. The reason why it has to so great an extent disappeared, is the great improvement in the manufacture and form of saddles, as it is solely caused by the bearing of the pommel or pinching from the sides of the saddle.

Although the term fistula can only be accurately applied to a particular form of wound, the disease which custom has designated fistulous withers is only truly so in its last stage. Where the saddle has bruised, inflammation is set up, and a tumour forms, which is very hot and tender to the touch; if noticed in time it may be dispersed by applying cooling lotions (pp. 9 & 37), sometimes aided by stimulating liniments (p. 24). If this treatment fails, and the tumour appears to go on to suppuration in spite of all efforts to disperse it, we must accept the inevitable, and giving up our previous efforts, endeavour, by fomentations and poultices to produce an early discharge of the collected pus, that it may not, as is its tendency, on account of the position of the tumour, drain downwards among healthy tissues, carrying disease with it, and forming deep fistulous sores most difficult to reach. The danger of this is so great that it is good policy to consult a practical man before the evil goes too far. Cases have not unfrequently occurred where, from neglect of proper treatment, the ulcers have extended downwards, and the matter appeared at the point of the shoulder and elbow, the bones becoming carious.

When the tumour is ripe it should be very freely opened with a knife, and the matter well pressed out, the discharge being encouraged by liberal fomentations and poultices, and the wound stimulated by an application of chloride of zinc.

Lotion for Stimulating Wounds.—Chloride of zinc, one and a half drachms to a pint of water.

A fistula fairly established can only be properly treated by a qualified veterinary surgeon, and owners should not permit the cruel experiments practised by ignorant pretenders.

Fits.—See Megrims.

Flatulent Colic.—See Colic.

Foot, Prick of the.—This occasionally, but rarely, occurs by the horse picking up a nail in travelling. As a rule it results from carelessness or accident in shoeing, for the most careful shoeing smith may have this mischance. It is very important to the horse and his owner that when such a misfortune does occur the smith should have the candour and moral courage to frankly name the matter, which unfortunately many have not, but endeavour to hide the truth, which only increases the evil, as by prompt dealing with, the worst results of the accident may be avoided. Some smiths are very careless, driving the nails home in a rough manner, without due caution, the result being that the point is driven into the quick, that is, into the fleshy substance of the sensitive laminæ, or into the soft horn lining the interior of the harder hoof. In the first instance the effect is more immediate; the horse will flinch; frequently there will be a little blood drawn, and lameness will be immediate, although it may be slight and of no duration. When the nail is driven into the soft horn between the hard hoof and the sensitive fibry substance, it will, by the action of the horse in walking, get bent and press on the sensitive parts, causing local inflammation, which, if not immediately attended to, will go on to suppuration or discharge of matter.

When lameness arises and prick of the foot is suspected, the shoe should at once be removed, look at the nails as they are drawn, and if one of them is moist, it reveals the injured spot; if it smells offensively matter has formed, and must be got rid of. If the spot cannot be detected in this way, feel round the foot with a pair of pincers as described in searching for a corn. When it is clear the horse has been pricked the foot should be placed in a bucket of warm water or a large poultice—of course, first having removed the shoe—the foot must be pared down, and a free opening made to allow of the discharge of matter. When it is slight, and the horse can bear the shoe and be gently worked, a piece of lint saturated with a mixture of Friar's balsam and camphorated oil should be pushed in, but in such a way as to be easily pulled out, the place cleaned, and a fresh piece put in. Barbadoes tar, which is semi-fluid, may be used instead of the Friar's balsam and camphorated oil. It is sometimes necessary in very bad cases to bleed from the toe; but this need not be done except when there is considerable local inflammation shown by the increased heat of the surrounding parts. When this is done put the foot into a bucket of water as warm as the horse can bear it, that the bleeding may be free, and the remedy quick and effectual, and in such a case it is good practice to give a few mashes and a mild dose of physic.

Foot Founder, Fever in the Feet, or Laminitis.—This disease is almost entirely confined to the fore feet; instances of all the feet being affected are of very rare occurrence, and even of the fore feet it often happens that only one is attacked. This local inflammation occasionally follows on the abatement of a more general inflammation, as of the lungs or bowels, and may also be produced by engorgement of the stomach with food of a heating nature. The most general cause, however, is the injudicious treatment of the horse by his rider or driver—over-exertion, and especially long and fast travelling on hard roads, particularly when the animal is brought home exhausted; therefore, on long journeys, and indeed, at all times, on hard roads in dry weather, extra care should be taken. The horse seized with fever in the feet may be left apparently all right at night, and the next morning found suffering intensely, as evidenced by his fidgety manner and frequent shiftings of the fore feet, which he throws out as far as possible, drawing the hind feet under him, that they may bear the weight of his body and relieve the affected fore feet, the fever or inflammation in which are evidently causing the poor beast excessive agony. If the feet are felt, the great unnatural heat of inflammation will at once be observed, and the arteries above may be felt throbbing violently.

The first thing to be done is the removal of the shoes, with as little fuss and pain to the animal as possible, for the sensitive part of the foot between the hoof and bone being in an inflamed state, the foot is very tender, and any rough handling causes exquisite and unnecessary pain. This may be better done if the feet are soaked an hour or two in warm water. On the shoes being removed, blood may be taken from the toe, and large poultices of bran or boiled turnips kept constantly applied; if hot poultices are used the heat should be kept up by frequently pouring over them fresh supplies of hot water. If cold poultices or lotions, the colder they are kept the better; and as they soon get hot against the inflamed surface, some of the cooling lotion (p. 9) should be used freely round the legs and poured over the poultice, or about 2oz. each of powdered sal ammoniac and saltpetre or common salt, dissolved in a bucket of water, may be similarly used. The horse should have gruel to drink, and his food consist of green food, mashes, &c. Of medicine, 1oz. of nitre a day may be given in his drink, and some of the fever medicine, a recipe for which will be found in the list of medicines at the end of the volume, or one of the fever balls (p. 23) may be given. In severe cases, however, it is very desirable that a veterinary surgeon should be consulted, who would probably administer remedies that would be unsafe in the hands of amateurs; but those who treat their own horses cannot be too mindful that gentle treatment and perfect quiet are essential to the animal's recovery. A horse that has suffered from inflammation in the feet should not be taken out of the stable too soon, and should at first be confined to the most gentle exercise, and that on soft turf.

Foot, Pumiced.—What is known as pumiced foot is oftenest seen in horses bred on low marshy lands, and in heavy draft horses with large wide feet, in which it is sure to be developed if used in town work, from the constant battering on the hard stones and pavement. It also follows founder, during the acute inflammation of which the horny plates which support the coffin bone get partially separated, and, losing their elasticity, fail in their duty, hence the coffin bone presses on the sole, which becomes convex. The front of the hoof falls in, showing a depression; the sole is flat, with rugged walls, and the whole hoof hard, dry, and brittle. All horses with flat wide feet and thin hoofs are subject to pumice, and its occurrence should in such cases be guarded against by applying softening preparations regularly as preventives; brushing over with cod oil or melted tallow answers well. In pumiced feet it has been recommended to blister the coronet, with a view to stimulate increased secretion of horn, but it is attended with very doubtful results. The best thing that can be done is to shoe with a broad webbed but thin shoe, and to dress the hoof regularly with a mixture of equal parts of Barbadoes tar, tallow, and glycerine, melted together, or with the hoof ointment (p. 15) prescribed for brittle hoof.

Founder, Foot.—See *Foot Founder*.

Fret.—See *Colic*.

G.

Gastritis, or Inflammation of the Stomach.—This is of comparatively rare occurrence in the horse, and is caused by poisoning, through accident or ignorance of the attendant. Horses will sometimes eat the leaves and twigs of the yew from off the tree, which suggests that there is already some derangement of the digestive organs, or the animal would not select as a food that which is harmful to him. Sometimes, however, the leaves and young shoots from the hedge clippings may be inadvertently left on the ground and picked up with the grass by the horse when grazing. This should be carefully avoided.

Many grooms and carters, more "knowing" than wise, give the horses under their charge drugs of a powerful and irritant character that should never be used except by the order and under the supervision of the veterinary surgeon. Most stablemen, however, have a reverence for nostrums, equal to their total want of knowledge of the power and character of the drugs of which they are compounded, and ignorance delights in secrecy and mystery; so that even the strong mineral acids, oil of vitriol, spirit of salt, and aquafortis are surreptitiously given to the master's horse to improve his appetite and appearance; whilst arsenic, savine, and cantharides each enter into various condition, coating, or worm powders in more or less repute with such people. If the disease is in an acute form, the symptoms will be more sudden in their appearance and more violent, the horse showing intense thirst, probably superpurgation, great pain, evidenced by the tucked-up belly, at which he kicks, or, in his rolling, as in colic, there may be violent straining and passing of mucus, and somtimes convulsions. If a veterinary surgeon is not within easy reach, give the following

Drench for Gastritis: Castor oil half a pint, bicarbonate of soda, ½oz.; laudanum, 2oz.; spirit of sulphuric ether, 1½oz., with a pint of gruel.

The veterinary should, however, be called in as soon as possible, as he might, on the spot, elicit facts which would suggest to him the cause, and, discovering the poison used, apply the best antidote.

A more chronic form of the disease may be induced by the noxious atmosphere of unclean and unventilated stables, combined with indifferent food and general want of attention, when the horse shows a vitiated appetite, greedily eating soiled litter, gnawing at manger, rack, &c., and devouring pieces of old mortar and other foreign and unnatural substances. This state should be counteracted by giving tonics and good food, but if the disease has progressed far it will require the skilled veterinary to deal with it.

Glanders.—See *Farcy*.

Grease.—This is one of the most filthy and loathsome diseases from which the horse suffers, and it is not merely discreditable, but most disgraceful to the intelligence and humanity of the owner, and to the character of the stableman for aptitude for his business, and honesty and industry in performing his duties, the disease being wholly preventible, and never occurring, except as the result of shameful ignorance of sanitary laws that may be said to be palpable to the grossest sense, or the culpable neglect of ordinary cleanliness and decent attention to the comfort of the animal under charge. That this is so may be proved by anyone at all observant who will ask himself where "Grease" is to be met with, and take the slightest trouble to answer the question practically. Assuredly he will not find it in the gentleman's stable, where the horse's health and comfort are studied, where a proper appreciation of the laws of health and the right of the four-footed servant to the consideration of man are shown in all the arrangements of the stable, and where the intelligent and active groom knows his duties, and is too proud alike of himself and his charge to neglect them.

The hotbeds of grease, as of many other horse diseases, are the dark and filthy dens where light and fresh air are as far as possible excluded, as though they carried destruction with them, where accumulated heaps of manure discharge gases that contaminate the air the horse is compelled to breathe, and where too often the poor animal's bedding, if he has any, is saturated, and he is forced to stand in pools of liquid manure, the exhalations from which have a harmful effect, both locally and generally. It is for the most part the aged and those debilitated with over work and indifferent food that suffer from grease, although an over stimulating and heated diet will tend to develop it where other circumstances are favourable to its presence. Among other causes of grease, clipping the hair from the heels, and thus depriving them of the warmth which nature placed the hair there to give, by preventing the rapid evaporation which takes place from a bare surface. Washing the feet in cold hard water, or, as is oftener done, dashing a pail or two of water over them and leaving them to dry as they like, tends to produce grease. When heavy draught horses are brought in muddy and wet, they should not be washed but relieved of the dirt as far as possible with a brush, and rubbed as dry as possible with wisps of straw, the horse will be far more comfortable than with his legs wet and cold, and grease and other untoward events obviated. Another source of grease is turning old horses out to grass in wet meadows in cold weather, and especially when pasture is scant; so that we see in every instance this is, in the strictest sense, a preventible disease, and as such, we repeat, a disgrace to the stable management where it occurs.

The first symptoms of grease are a scurfiness and itching of the legs. The scurfiness can be seen in grooming, and the itchiness is plainly indicated by the horse frequently stamping his feet on the ground and rubbing the back of one leg with the other. The hair begins to stand out, cracked heels succeed, and the fetlocks become tumified; a discharge takes place, which may be seen standing on the hairs in drops; this rapidly increases, as does the swelling and the cracks on the heel, and the abhorrent smell, so peculiar to the discharge in this disease, becomes intensified as the discharge increases, lameness sets in, and if the disease is not checked and mastered granulations appear in bunches, and the horse suffers great pain from the slightest contact of the parts with the straw bedding, &c.

The first thing to be done in case of grease is to diligently search for the cause which produced it, and which will encourage and intensify it and retard progress towards recovery. These causes will not be far to seek, and should be at once removed. In the scurfy stage, when increased heat and swelling are beginning, wash the legs well with soap and warm water, drying carefully afterwards; then apply constantly bandages saturated with this lotion:

Lotion for Grease: Extract of lead 1oz., tincture of arnica 1oz., water 18oz., mixed.

Two or three bandages should be at hand, and frequently changed, a they get hot very quickly. If the heels have cracked, and there is much of the offensive discharge, apply very large poultices, changing them as soon as they get at all cold, and dress the legs with the following between the changes :

Lotion for Cracked Heels : Take chloride of zinc two drachms, glycerine two ounces, tincture of arnica 1oz., tincture of myrrh 1oz., water to make 1½ pints.

In the chronic stages caustics or the firing iron must be resorted to, and when the granulations above referred to have formed, they have to be removed by the knife, but these are operations requiring the advice and assistance of the veterinary surgeon.

When grease appears in a horse in good condition, he should at once have a dose of physic—of course having been first prepared by mashes— also 1oz. of nitre in his mash. During grease the horse should not be worked at all if the case is severe, but gentle exercise is always beneficial. The food should be good, but not of a heating nature : Old beans and good heavy oats, but with these carrots, and clover in season. On recovery the horse should have a course of tonics—the tonic powders (p. 53) will answer very well, adding to each dose ½oz. of powdered resin and ½oz. of nitre. Or the following prescribed by Mayhew may be substituted for the tonic powders :

Tonic Draught : Take liquor arsenicalis ½oz., tincture of muriate of iron 6 drachms, strong ale or stout 1 pint, to be given night and morning.

Grease, Molten.—See *Molten Grease.*
Gripes.—See *Colic.*
Gullion.—See *Colic.*

H.

Heart Disease.—This is quite incurable, and, moreover, its existence is most difficult to determine, and but few outside the profession are able to decide with any certainty whether the horse is or is not under its influence. Should there be any reason to suspect its presence from the haggard and constantly anxious look of the horse, and from any irregularity or unusual action of the heart when carefully listened to by placing the ear against it on the lower part of the chest on the left side, it will be well to have a veterinary surgeon to confirm or remove doubts. As death from this disease is always sudden, and most likely to occur when the horse is undergoing great exertion, as when ridden or driven fast, there is great danger of accidents arising ; therefore, when assured that the disease is established, there being no certain symptoms of immediate death, but which last invariably occurs as a surprise, it is better either to destroy life or keep the animal to slow and easy work, by which human life would not be subjected to danger.

Hidebound.—The condition of the horse familiarly known as hidebound is in every case the result of culpable neglect of his wants by his owner. It arises from exposure in cold wet weather, in bare pasture, or open shed, or straw-yard, where no protection is provided, and accompanied by an insufficiency of food, or food of such quality that it fails to yield sufficient healthy sustenance. Horses subjected to such treatment—and particularly those that have been accustomed to have their wants properly supplied and their comforts studied—soon present a miserable and dejected appearance, with the belly down, and the skin, foul and dirty, is harsh and tightly stretched all over the body, having lost all its elasticity, with its softness and gloss.

When the cause is so apparent the remedy is not far to seek. A return to good wholesome, nutritious diet, not, however, too suddenly, but gradually, introducing corn and beans, with a mash and a few cut roots, will restore the animal to his wonted health. With the general debility, which more or less attends on a state of hidebound, it is highly probable the digestive organs have suffered in their constant attempts to assimilate sufficient nutriment from the rubbish with which to stay the gnawings of hunger, the stomach has been constantly crammed; it will, therefore, be well to assist the horse's recovery to perfect health by a course of tonics, combining with them such medicines as have a direct action on the skin. The following powders will be found useful:

Tonic Powders.—Pure sulphate of iron, 3oz.; powdered gentian, 6oz.; ground ginger, 3oz.; ground aniseed, 6oz.; mix and divide into twelve powders, and give one daily mixed with the food and slightly damped.

Give at the same time 1 drachm of Fowler's solution of arsenic night and morning, either in water after the feed, or mixed with a little water and sprinkled over the corn.

Hock, Capped.—See *Capped Hock.*

Hydrophobia.—This terrible disease is comparatively rare, and never exists except as the result of contagion from the bite of some rabid animal, generally cat or dog. The symptoms vary; sometimes there is an entire loss of appetite, and in other cases the appetite is ravenous, and at the same time vitiated, everything within reach being greedily consumed, even to the most soiled litter; there is great nervous excitement, and the animal becomes wild and dangerous. As science has hitherto failed to discover a cure for this frightful malady the poor sufferer should, by a well directed shot or some other speedy means, be delivered from his great sufferings.

I.

Inflammation of the Bowels.—See *Enteritis.*
Inflammation of the Eye.—See *Ophthalmia.*
Inflammation of the Kidneys.—See *Kidneys.*

Inflammation of the Lungs.—See *Catarrh, Cough,* and *Pneumonia.*
Inflammation of the Stomach.—See *Gastritis.*
Influenza. — This disease appears to be of an epidemic character, attacking animals' simultaneously over a wide district; young animals are for the most part the subjects of attack, and it is generally most prevalent in the spring of the year. The first symptom indicating influenza likely to be observed by the groom or owner is the very rapid loss of strength, which is an invariable accompaniment or result of the disease. On examination the white of the eye will be seen to have a yellowish tinge, and the whole eye dull; the pulse is feeble but wiry, the lining membrane of the nostrils pale; a thick copious discharge from the nose sets in, with frequent cough and occasionally sore throat; the whole frame becomes affected; sometimes local swellings occur; and not uncommonly the legs swell, and there is considerable heat and fever in the feet, with lameness. As a rule the bowels are constipated, and the great debility of the animal precludes the use of purgatives. When influenza is first discovered the horse should be placed in the most comfortable loose box at command, where he can breathe fresh air without being exposed to draughts or subjected to sudden changes of temperature. This is a disease where good nursing and kind attention is of quite as much value as medicines; the horse must be made as comfortable as possible, and all his wants regularly attended to with little fuss and much kindness, which the sympathetic nature of the horse will fully appreciate. Where, as is generally the case, the bowels are constipated, this must be overcome by very gentle laxatives, such as linseed or olive oil, assisted by gruel mashes with stewed linseed, boiled carrots, &c., and in some cases aided by back raking (as already described, p. 33). To encourage the nasal discharge, reduce the fever, and as likely to give special relief in cases where there is sore throat, the following electuary should be made, and a tablespoonful of it placed on the tongue at intervals of a few hours:

Electuary for Sore Throat. — Take powdered chlorate of potash 4oz., powdered gum guaiacum 2oz., powdered gum acacia 2oz., powdered liquorice 4oz., powdered opium ½oz.; let these be very carefully mixed and made into an electuary by the addition of 8oz. of honey and 8oz. of oxymel of squills.

One of the principal objects to be kept in view in treating a horse with influenza is to keep up the strength, which very rapidly fails in all instances, and this feature of the disease must be promptly met by the administration of stimulants such as sulphuric and nitric ether, spirit of sal volatile, &c.: these may be given from the first.

Stimulant in Influenza.—Dose, 1oz. of sulphuric ether, ½oz. spirit of nitrous ether, and 1oz. of laudanum, given in a pint of gruel night and morning.

As the nasal discharge increases ale or porter should be substituted for the gruel. Artificial stimulants must not, however, be entirely depended on, the animal should be coaxed to eat strengthening and easily assimilated food, by giving a little and often, never leaving any before it untouched; strong gruel, mashes with carrots and linseed, and tea made from good hay, a little good hay, freshly bruised oats, and roots may also be allowed if the animal will take them; exercise must be permitted gradually to the convalescent, and even a return of appetite must not be indulged too freely till recovery is assured, and exercise or work resumed.

Indigestion.—Indigestion in the horse may be the result of inflammation of the stomach, but more frequently it is directly caused by irregular feeding, and especially by the very long fasts to which this noble animal is often, through culpable thoughtlessness, subjected to.

There are but few men comparatively who either drive or ride who would wilfully perpetrate the cruelty that is often thus practised except from inconsiderateness, and all should remember that—

> Ill is wrought by want of thought,
> As well as want of heart.

If the fact were constantly borne in mind that the horse has a very small stomach, which must be often replenished to enable him to supply the constant wants of his great frame, the waste of which must be constantly rebuilt, the master would not forget the pint of oatmeal for the horse when he called for his own biscuit and sherry; and in the hunting field, or on long fatiguing journeys, a few biscuits carried in the pocket will prove acceptable and valuable to the horse.

These long fasts exhaust the horse so that on reaching the stable the appetite, which hours ago was ravenous, has disappeared; he is too exhausted to eat, and if he does the stomach fails in its work, and the food continues to be passed in an undigested form.

When a horse after a journey refuses to eat, he may be roused by giving the following drench:

Drench for Stimulating Appetite.—Compound spirit of sulphuric ether 1oz., tincture of ginger ½oz., and tincture of cardamoms 1½oz., given in a pint of gruel.

In cases of indigestion the food must be studied—small mashes, clover, roots, with bruised oats, split beans sparingly given, and good upland hay. It is better to give the feeds often than allow a returning appetite to gorge the stomach, therefore divide the four daily feeds into six, and a small tablespoonful of the following cordial powder sprinkled over each feed, and the whole slightly damped will coax the appetite, and aid digestion:

Cordial Powder.—Pimento berries, powdered, 4oz., ground ginger 2oz., ground carraways 4oz., powdered liquorice 2oz., common salt 1oz., mixed carefully, and kept in a dry place.

K.

Kidneys, Inflammation of the.—This disease, which is not infrequent, is of a very serious character. It is always accompanied by intense fever, pain over the loins, as seen when pressure is applied there; there is constant attempts to pass urine, which, when successful, is in small quantities, and high coloured, or thick and viscid. The horse stands in a straddling manner, as in other diseases of the urinary organs.

The disease with which it is most likely to be confounded is inflammation of the bladder, and this can be decided by passing the hand up the rectum very carefully, when, as the hand gradually nears the diseased organ, great heat will be felt, and much sensitiveness shown by the horse. The operation should, therefore, be performed with great caution, both on account of the acute pain that rashness may cause the horse, and the danger to the operator from the animal becoming restive.

The principal cause giving rise to inflammation of the kidneys, is feeding on new oats or kiln-dried oats, mow-burnt hay, and the giving of powerful diuretics. The treatment consists in at once bleeding and getting the bowels freely opened by the use of clysters and a purge; strong mustard poultices should be applied across the loins, and warm fomentations kept up constantly; half a drachm of calomel and one drachm of powdered opium should be given night and morning; aconite is useful, but only safe in professional hands. The food should consist of thick gruel, boiled linseed, mashes, &c., and during existence of the disease the patient should have as much of the more liquid food warm as he can be induced to take.

Knees, Broken.—See *Broken Knees.*

L.

Laminitis.—See *Foot Founder.*

Lampas.—This is scarcely worthy to be styled a disease, being no more so than is the swelling of a child's gums when teething—it has, nevertheless, been made much of by grooms and farriers, who, far too cunning to be taught, continue, in their ignorance and inhumanity, to inflict the torture of the hot iron to reduce a swelling which, left alone and the dictates of common sense followed in feeding, would very quickly disappear.

Across the roof of the horse's mouth there are ridges or "bars," as they are more usually termed, and lampas is nothing more than a temporary swelling of these "bars" till they rise to a level with the teeth, so that the animal cannot chew hard food, and constantly drops the corn from his mouth unmasticated. When this is noticed "Boxer" is declared to be "off his feed;" the groom looks for and finds lampas, and pats himself on the back as an amazingly clever fellow for having done so. If he would only stop there no harm would be done; but too often his conceit and ignorance, unchecked as it should be by the intelligence of the master, indulges itself in conspiring with the farrier, as ignorant as himself, in torturing the poor dumb beast well nigh to madness with the lampas iron, causing inexpressible pain, and frequently causing damage to the horse for life.

Lampas is almost if not entirely restricted to young horses, and is probably a mild sympathetic inflammation of the parts consequent on the development of the teeth, and it is often directly caused by a sudden change from soft food to dry corn. No medicinal treatment is necessary, simply feed on soft food, mashes, with boiled linseed, steamed carrots, and a few oats softened in the same way added, and nature will do her work quickly and well. Above all, permit no meddling; the barbarous practices referred to must die with the spread of knowledge, but such ignorant prejudices are hard to kill, and it behoves every intelligent horseowner to assist in stamping them out.

Larvæ in the Skin.—The presence of these pests is known by the appearance of small lumps like very diminutive molehills chiefly on the back, and often supposed to be and called "heat lumps." They are found on horses that have been out to grass in the summer; they appear in the course of the winter, increasing in size as spring advances, and cause very considerable annoyance and so much pain from pressure of the saddle as to make the horse restive, and indeed unfit for work. These lumps are caused by the presence of a grub or maggot, which gets possession in the following singular manner: When in the fields in summer the horse is surrounded with insects of many various kinds, and by them subjected to much annoyance, and I may say, indignity, for, as explained in the article on Bots, they not only annoy him, but deposit their eggs on him, and make him the nursery of their future broods. The eggs, producing the larvæ at present referred to, are deposited on the back and sides; and when, by aid of the warmth of the horse's body, a little worm is hatched from the egg, it bores its way into the skin, where the bigger it grows the more mischief it does. Mr. Mayhew, in his "Illustrated Horse Doctor," has given an excellent engraving of this little pest, and shows the ill effects he produces. At the top of the lump formed is a small dark spot, being the hole through which the larva receives the air necessary to its existence; to stop this up with tallow, beeswax, or any such substance is to ensure the death of the worm, but that only renders the condition of the horse worse, as the body of the maggot putrifies in the sac which incloses it, and the abscess is thereby enlarged and inflammation set up, which may affect materially the whole system; the best plan, therefore, is to open the abscess with a lancet at the hole at the top, and then the maggot can be squeezed out. When it has been removed, and all matter pressed out, sponge the part with warm water and apply a little Friar's balsam to the puncture.

Lice.—Horses are sometimes infested with these troublesome and disgusting parasites, but only those that are kept in a filthy state, half starved, and generally neglected; and, if a properly seen-to horse suffers, it is from accidental contact with his less fortunate fellow. I have seen them literally swarming on a young animal just brought from grass, and horses so troubled are very apt to be hide bound, and therefore require good feeding and extra care. When the lice infest the tail they cause so much irritation that the horse will rub it bare; and I believe there is some difference between the lice there and those that infest the body. Turpentine applied to the tail will destroy them, and as these, like other insects, breathe through their skin, Mayhew recommends smearing the whole body of the horse with oil or grease to suffocate the lice, and afterwards washing the grease off. "Stonehenge" recommends that dry white precipitate in powder should be rubbed into the coat, and in a few hours brushed out, muzzling the horse in the meantime to prevent him licking it. This is a certain cure, but it is rather dangerous to use in such large quantities, as it flies about and gets into the mouth and nose of the person who is applying it, and besides that it is very expensive. I think the following wash will be found thoroughly effective, easier to use, and less costly:

Wash for Destroying Lice.—Take of stavesacre seeds, well bruised, 2lb.; quassia chips, 1lb.; soft water, 4 gallons; pearl ashes, 2oz.

Boil slowly down to three gallons, strain it, and wash the horse with it, using a little plain or soft soap; let it saturate the coat to the skin, and remain in the coat a minute or two, when, if necessary, plain water may be added to finish the washing. I need scarcely say that after such a sousing the horse must be rubbed perfectly dry.

Looseness.—See *Diarrhœa*.

Lungs, Inflammation of.—See *Catarrh, Cough,* &c

M.

Mad Staggers.—See *Staggers*.

Maggots in the Skin.—See *Larvæ in the Skin*.

Mallenders and Sallenders.—Mallenders is the name applied to a scurfy, sometimes scabby, eruption in the bend of the fore legs at the back of the knee. Sallenders is the name given to a similar eruption located in front of the hock. The first appearance is dry scurf, rendering the hair rough, hard, and dirty looking, and, if unchecked, the skin cracks, and a sore is formed, troublesome to heal and discharging foul matter. This affection, for mallenders and sallenders are identical in character, is produced by foulness of blood, requiring physic and alterative medicines, or, as is often the case, it is the result of the idleness and neglect of the groom. If the proper course be at once taken it will not go beyond its first stage. Wash with warm water, dry thoroughly, and apply two or three times a day the following:

Lead Liniment.—Goulard's extract of lead 2oz., olive oil 10oz., mixed.

At the same time alterative tonics should be given; the following powders would be suitable:

Alterative Tonic Powders.—Sulphate of iron 4oz., black sulphuret of antimony and powdered nitre each 3oz., flowers of sulphur 6oz., ground carraway seeds ½lb.

Give a tablespoonful in the corn and chaff night and morning. In obstinate cases give in addition 2 drachms of Fowler's solution of arsenic, added to a little water, and sprinkled over the food, and substitute for the lead and oil liniment the following ointment:

Mercurial Ointment.—Powdered camphor 2 drachms, strong mercurial ointment ½oz., lard 2oz., mix and rub in a little three times a day.

When the skin has cracked, and a discharge from the sores is going on, poultices are useful before applying the ointment, which should then be made weaker by the addition of another ounce of lard.

Mange.—Mange is a term applied to several skin diseases in the lower animals, accompanied with excessive itching. In the horse true mange is caused by the presence of an insect too small to be seen by the naked eye, except in the strongest light, when the living specks can be detected by their motion. Under the microscope they are revealed in all their native ugliness, and, as Mayhew puts it, "resembling a deformed crab" in their repulsiveness. "Stonehenge" suggests that some forms of mange are dependent on a vegetable parasite of fungoid character, and supports this by the following argument:—"No disease being more contagious than this, nor more difficult to eradicate from a stable when once it has broken out, rather favours its vegetable origin, the seeds of all kinds of fungus being most difficult to destroy." Whether mange is ever developed spontaneously I am unable to discuss, but there can be no doubt that dirt and neglect are a direct encouragement to it, but the very large majority of cases can be directly traced to contagion from contact with diseased animals, and in those comparatively few cases where the origin cannot be clearly traced it can be shrewdly guessed at. The most likely places to contract the disease are bait stables of the lower class, grazing fields where the animals are taken in promiscuously, or from the visits of a diseased horse to the home stable. The disease is so "catching" that all harness, shafts of vehicles, stalls, and posts with which a suspected animal has been in contact should be thoroughly cleansed and disinfected before a sound horse is allowed to go near them. Mange almost invariably first appears in the mane, the first symptom to attract attention being the intense itching, proved by the horse constantly rubbing himself. If the mane is closely examined it will be found scurfy, a slight discharge oozes from the skin and dries on the hair, which is easily pulled out, and as the disease proceeds it falls off or gets rubbed off in the animal's endeavours to relieve the itching; the skin ultimately becomes puckered and furrowed, a discharge more or less exuding from the furrows. It rapidly spreads along the head, neck, and back, and the poor animal, getting no rest, loses condition. Anyone may determine by examination and attention to the above symptoms whether his horse has mange, the only disease likely to be mistaken for it being surfeit; but in that there is not the intense itching, nor the watery discharge, but merely a quantity of small bumps or heat spots, which generally appear very suddenly.

The treatment of mange must depend on the condition of the horse; if gross and fat he should have a physic ball once a week, and the quantity of corn reduced, giving green food if obtainable, or carrots; he should also have alteratives, the powders prescribed for mallenders (p. 58) will answer well, but the sulphate of iron must be left out; but in the case of poor, ill-conditioned animals, generous feeding must be adopted and tonics added to the alteratives—that is, the sulphate of iron must be retained in the powders, and an equal quantity of powdered gentian added. The local applications recommended for mange are innumerable, most of them exceedingly nasty, and nearly all contain very dangerous poisons, such as arsenic, corrosive sublimate, hellebore, strong mercurial ointment, &c., mixed up with some stinking fish oil. This is altogether unnecessary, as more efficient means of cure, and much more cleanly can be had. Any of the following may be used without danger:—

Dressings for Mange.—Take pure crystallised carbolic acid ½oz., glycerine 8oz., laudanum 2oz., water 16oz.; mix and apply with a rag three or four times a day. Or take flowers of sulphur 8oz., powdered nitrate of potash 1oz., lard 1lb., spirit of turpentine ½oz.; thoroughly mix and rub into the parts affected twice a day; but a still cleaner, and I can, from personal experience of it, say a most effectual cure, is the cure for mange, made by Spratt's Patent Dog Biscuit Manufacturers, and it is entirely free from poison.

Whatever dressing is selected, its application should be preceded by a thorough cleansing of the parts, either by brushing or washing; but in any but very cold weather I prefer the latter, adding 2oz. of carbonate of potash to a bucket of water, and using soft soap. All the stall posts, manger, and every place the horse can have rubbed against must be thoroughly cleansed with soap and boiling water, and brushed over with the mange lotion, so as to thoroughly eradicate the disease from the stable; but with good well-ventilated stables, and proper attention to feeding and grooming, this foul disease should never appear.

As mange is very unmanageable and difficult to eradicate, and seems sometimes to yield to one remedy, sometimes to another, perhaps it may be as well for me to add a few more recipes for the cure of it, all of which have their advocates, so that those who unfortunately have an animal to treat for it may have variety to choose from. I, however, would not look further for a cure than in those already given, adding only in cases that seemed to resist the persistent use of them a very strong tincture of stavesacre seeds, which should be made according to the following formula:

Tincture of Stavesacre.—Take of the seeds of stavesacre (*Delphinium*

Staphysagria) bruised 1lb., water 1½ pints, boil slowly down to half a pint or rather less, strain, and having pressed the seeds, place them in a percolator, and pass through it rectified spirit of wine till half a pint is obtained, mix this with the decoction, add ½ pint of glycerine, and apply to the mangy parts, thoroughly saturating the skin.

Petroleum or rock oil or paraffin is often used with effect, and leaves the coat smooth and glossy. But where the skin is broken both this and the preparation of stavesacre are too severe, causing very great and unnecessary pain.

Stavesacre Ointment.—An ointment made of 2 oz. of finely powdered stavesacre to ½lb. of lard sometimes proves useful; it should be well rubbed in several times a day.

The following wash is recommended in extreme cases by "Stonehenge," who at the same time points out its dangerous nature as a powerful poison, a caution I wish to enforce by repetition:

Hellebore Wash.—Take powdered white hellebore, 8oz., water 3 quarts, boil gently till the whole is reduced to 2 quarts, and then add 1 drachm of corrosive sublimate.

This wash should be well brushed into the skin with a paint brush, and no more should be used than will suffice to touch over the diseased parts.

Iodide of sulphur is also used with good results—it is applied either in solution or in the form of ointment; the latter, which should always be made fresh as wanted, is as follows:

Iodide of Sulphur Ointment.—Iodide of sulphur, reduced to a fine powder, two parts; spermaceti ointment, fourteen parts; thoroughly mixed.

The following liniment for mange and wash for mange, are taken from Mayhew's work, "The Illustrated Horse Doctor:"

Liniment for Mange.—Animal glycerine, eight parts; creosote, one part; oil of turpentine, two parts; oil of juniper, one part; mix all together, shake well, and use.

Wash for Mange.—Corrosive sublimate, 1dr.; spirits of wine, 1oz.; tobacco, 1oz.; boiling water, 1qt.; to make, dissolve the corrosive sublimate in the spirits of wine; soak the tobacco in the boiling water; when cold mix the two solutions."

Mayhew points out the danger of the above wash, and says he cannot sincerely recommend it. It is very poisonous.

To conclude, the following is a pretty fair sample of the horrors (i.e., disgusting, and dangerous messes resorted to by ignorant quacks) and others, and he is in great reverence as a profound mystery. It is needless to say that the ill effects too often following the use of such absurd and dangerous nostrums is rarely attributed to their real cause, and a professional man is called in and he is sure to be more or less severely unskilful treatment, his opinion would probably by people stupid enough to trust the well being of their horses to those more ignorant than themselves, be put down to personal spite or professional pique. Ointment for mange.—Black brimstone ¼lb., flowers of brimstone ¾lb. (generally written floury), black hellebore 1oz., white hellebore 4oz., corrosive sublimate ¼oz. (generally called supplement), blue unction (mercurial ointment) 1oz., spirits of tar quarter-pint, whale oil half-pint, oil of origanum 1oz., hog's lard 1½lb., mixed. Stupid and dangerous alike as the above is it is an improvement on many of the nostrums chemists are requested to compound, and which, to their credit, they never do, quietly making a better and a safer article instead, knowing it would be as absurd to reason on the subject with the horse as the horse doctor, and for this wise discretion on the part of the chemist, gentlemen, farmers, and others have to be thankful, as it is the saving of the lives of many valuable animals.

Megrims.—The disease known as megrims is a temporary pressure on the brain producing partial or entire insensibility; it may result from pressure of the collar, extra exertion, or possibly sometimes from the excessive heat of the sun, or the cause may be so remote as to be undiscoverable to us. The fit comes on suddenly and without warning, and very frequently when the animal is in harness; and especially is the horse predisposed to megrims likely to have an attack if driven with a tight bearing rein, which prevents the natural free action of the head. In very slight attacks the horse stops, throws up his head, and, staring round stupidly for a short time, recovers, and is ready to go on as if nothing unusual had occurred. In severer cases he will rear, or, suddenly turning round, rush, in defiance of control, into danger, finally falling down, where he will remain from one to probably ten minutes, according to the severity of the attack. In such a case the head should be kept down, the harness loosened, and the horse not allowed to arise until the driver is assured he has fully recovered consciousness and the animal should be soothed by kind word and action; all noisy bluster and excitement, although it may spring from good intentions, is to be condemned. In very bad cases it may be advisable to attempt relief by bleeding on the spot, or as soon as the horse can be got to his stable, when the bleeding should be from the neck vein, and if the horse is of full habit, he should be prepared with mashes, and receive a physic ball. Entire rest is also essential, with gentle leading exercise only. Although there are instances where a horse has had but one fit of megrims, the general rule is that they are recurring, and therefore unusual care in riding and driving must be exercised, as from the suddenness of the attack the rider or driver is placed in great jeopardy. As preventives the suitability of the collar should be looked to, the bearing rein abolished; the horse should not be forced to over-exertion, nor unduly and improperly excited, and his general health assured by a judicious system of feeding, grooming, and exercise, and by providing a stable of sufficient size, and properly ventilated. This latter is a most important point, to which too little attention is paid. Every writer on hygiene lays it down as a law that men cannot continue to live in health in houses where there is less than a given number of cubic feet of air for each, and provision for the renewal of fresh air, as it is used and becomes vitiated; but the horse is too often lodged as if the laws of nature could be set at defiance with impunity, very much to the owner's loss in money, although he may be unable to see it.

Molten Grease is spoken of as a special disease in all old books of farriery, and by the uneducated horse doctor of the present day, the theory being that the inward fat of the horse becomes liquified, and is carried off by the bowels, or, as one old writer puts it, " As for the inward grease which is in the stomach bag and guts, if when once it gets melted it be not removed by art, medicine, and good feeding, it putrifies and breeds those mortal diseases which inevitably destroy the horse, though it be half a year or three-quarters of a year after, and this is generally the source of fevers, surfeits, consumptions, &c., and such other distempers which carry off infinite numbers of horses." In a similar way swelled legs were, and are still, by some ignorant people, accounted for by the melting of the fat nearer to the surface. The writer quoted above, in his instructions how to order a hunter—many of which are thoroughly sensible—says: " Lay your hand on the lower part of the horse's short ribs near the flank, and if you feel his fat to be soft and tender, and to yield, as it were, under your hand, then you may be confident it is unsound, and that the least violent labour or travel will dissolve it, which, being dissolved ere it is hardened by good diet, if it be not then removed by scouring, the fat or grease belonging to the outward parts of the body will fall down into his heels and so cause goutiness and swelling. I need not trouble you with the outward signs of this distemper, they are evident to the eye; but every groom can inform you when a horse is said to have the grease fallen into his heels, yet may be he cannot instruct you in the cause why travel disperseth it for a time, and when the horse is cold it returns with more violence than before. The reason, therefore, is this: the grease which by indiscreet exercise and negligence in keeping is melted and fallen into his legs, standing still in the stable cools and congeals, and so unites itself with other ill humours which flow to the affected part, so that they stop the natural circulation of the blood and cause inflammations and swellings, as aforesaid; but travel produceth warmth in the limbs, thaws as it were the congealed humours, and disperses them throughout the body in general, till rest gives them the opportunity to unite and settle again." I have given the above quotations because I know that those who trust the treatment of their ailing horses to grooms and farriers must often hear, as I have heard, some such attempts to account for diseases that were not understood. And such opinions given as above expressed, and with less show of reason, should be a warning that those who thus empirically account for a disease cannot be safe persons to trust with its treatment. The disease which is called among the vulgar molten grease, is a chronic or severe diarrhœa, accompanied with more or less fever, and the discharge which was taken for liquid fat is the mucus which lines and lubricates the intestines, and should be treated as diarrhœa, to which article I refer readers.

N.

Nasal Gleet.—See *Gleet*, also *Catarrh*.

Nasal Polypus.—See *Polypus*.

Navicular Disease.—The existence of this disease is difficult to determine by the amateur; even the skilled veterinary surgeon at times finds it difficult to distinguish between that and other causes of lameness arising from affections of that most beautiful but complex piece of mechanism the foot of the horse. The navicular bone, which is placed behind and between the lower pastern and coffin bone, and rests on the perforans tendon, although of small size, is one of the most important parts of the horse's structure; it comes into play in every motion, and its free action is assisted by a synovial sac, which, placed between the bone and tendon, acts the part of lubricator, and renders motion free and easy. The cause of navicular disease is from sudden pressure by a stone, or some such uneven surface on which the horse may tread, and which first injuring the frog and the tendon referred to bruises the bone; the frog and tendon, each flexible, soon recover, but the injury to the bone remains permanent. Navicular is a disease most often seen in high class horses and free goers. It makes its appearance suddenly and apparently at the time without cause, and its treatment by an amateur is still more difficult than its diagnosis, and it is much the best plan in cases of lameness, where the cause is not self-evident, to at once take the advice of the best veterinary surgeon at command. If prompt measures are adopted there is a chance of the disease being cured, and, at all events, by a severing of the nerve, which the learned call neurotomy, the poor horse will be saved from inconceivable suffering, a result which humane owners of horses will always consider. The acute pain arising from disease of the navicular bone Mayhew brings home to the conception of all by comparing it to "twenty toothaches compressed into one agony," and to relieve, or, still better, to prevent such misery, should be a first consideration with, as it is a first duty of, every horse owner. As a preventative of navicular disease, a leather sole is recommended, especially for horses used on hard and macadamised roads.

Needle Worms.—See *Worms*.

Nephritis.—See *Kidneys, Inflammation of.*

Nerving, or Neurotomy, is the operation of dividing the nerves; it is practised in painful affections of the feet, such as navicular disease; but it can only be trusted to those skilled in the use of the knife and who have a thorough knowledge of the anatomy of the parts.

Nettle Rash.—Horses are subject to nettle rash, which consists of diffused swellings in the skin, raised to the thickness of half a crown, and of variable extent; it is generally caused by exposure to sudden changes of weather. For fuller particulars see *Surfeit.*

O.

Ophthalmia, or Inflammation of the Eye.—This is either simple and temporary, or specific and chronic—in the one instance a local affection only, in the other it becomes constitutional, affecting the whole system. Simple inflammation of the eye is either the result of an accident occurring to the horse in play or from some foreign body, as a speck of dust or a hay seed from the rack lodging in the eye, or, as is too frequently the case, from the lash of the whip cruelly applied to such a sensitive organ, or it may be the result of a cold. When a fly, dirt, or any irritating substance lodges in the eye, it causes tears to flow, which, as it were, wash it downwards. The lachrymal gland being situated at the top corner of the eye, the hard or third eyelid being projected by the same excitement of the parts, produced by the pain, scoops up the offending particle, and, the cause being removed, the effect ceases; but in the case of a hay seed, for instance, the hard, sharp point may have stuck fast, and prove too obstinate to be removed by the means Nature has provided, when man's help is called for, and it may be necessary to extract the seed by means of small tweezers or the point of a penknife. Where the irritation has been so great as to produce much inflammation, and when it is the result of cold, or a blow or lash, it may be necessary to give a dose of physic and 1½oz. of sweet spirit of nitre, with 1oz. of laudanum as a drench in a quart of gruel; but generally speaking a lighter diet than usual, consisting of mashes, steamed corn gruel made with hay, and the addition of carrots, or clover, or vetches, when obtainable, will obviate the use of medicine, which is always to be avoided when it can be done without. One of the following lotions should be very freely used to the eye affected, and to both where, as is often the case, the other shows sympathetic inflammation:

Eye Lotions.—Take sulphate of zinc 2 scruples, laudanum 1oz., water 8oz., mix; or take a dozen poppy heads of fair size, crush them and boil slowly for twenty minutes; strain the decoction, add to it 1oz. of Goulard's extract of lead, previously mixed with 1oz. of spirit of wine, and soft water to make the whole 1 quart.

Having placed a folded linen cloth across both eyes, keep it constantly well wetted with the above.

Specific Ophthalmia is much more difficult to manage, and it is more direful in its results, generally ending, sooner or later, with the loss of one or both eyes. It comes on much in the same way as simple inflammation, only all the symptoms are more pronounced, especially the intolerance of light, which is present in both diseases; and, in addition, there is a

E

general disturbance of the system, which is the main thing the surgeon will look for to enable him to form an opinion. It is safe practice for the horse owner, when the symptoms of inflammation of the eye are unusually severe, and do not quickly yield to the remedies given above, at once to consult a skilled veterinarian without delay. Above all things, do not permit harsh measures of cruelty, under which farriers attempt to cloak, but which really display, their ignorance, one of which is to cut away the hair from lids which have, of course, suffered with other parts of the eye, and from their enlarged and red appearance are held to be the cause, instead of one of the suffering membranes. Among the causes of ophthalmia are sudden change to warm stables and high living: and when this cause is known, bleeding, physic and mashes substituted for corn may prevent it going beyond the first stage. Often the cause is small, hot, and ill-ventilated stables, where there is not sufficient air to supply the wants of the horse, and the atmosphere is further vitiated by the exhalations, especially the free ammonia discharged from dung and urine. These are preventible causes, and to prevention and the more simple attempt at cure of the disease in its incipient stages the owner's personal efforts should be limited.

Over-reach.—Fast horses, and especially those that in their natural step considerably overlap with their hind feet the ground covered by the fore feet, are most liable to the injury termed over-reach. Such horses, when tried, may be heard to click, the fore foot not being removed quick enough, the toe of the hind shoe knocks or clicks against the shoe of the fore foot; it is at such times or in a gallop across stiff ground which holds the foot that the evil is likely to take place, the hind foot catching the heel of the fore foot a blow, resulting in an injury likely to produce suppuration, and, if not judiciously treated, ending in quittor or false quarter. The treatment required is to (with care and gentleness) clean the wound, and if it is a simple clean cut apply to it with a soft brush or camel's hair pencil equal parts of tincture of arnica and tincture of matico, mixed, afterwards binding the wound up with a linen bandage, with the part of it immediately covering the wound well wetted with a mixture in equal parts of Friar's balsam and camphorated oil; this must be changed in two or three days, and if matter has formed apply to it the lotion of chloride of zinc (p. 47). Where the wound is a torn and ragged one, bathe it with this lotion:

Lotion for Ragged Wounds.—Sulphate of copper 2dr., vinegar 2oz., water 7oz., apply daily, keeping the wound covered with the balsam and camphorated oil.

P.

Paralysis.—Horses, like all our domestic animals, are liable to affections of the nervous system involving a partial or total loss of power. Partial paralysis is most frequently met with. Total paralysis when it occurs follows as a sequence to some violent disease, and is incurable. Even partial paralysis is very doubtful of cure, but it may often be alleviated, although the animal is never perfectly restored to his former state, or made fit for his previous employment; for it is generally the fast and showy horse, and the overworked omnibus or post horse, that is the victim of the disease. It is often produced by a fall under a heavy load, or in leaping, &c., or by other direct injury to the spine, in the region of the back or loins. Paralysis in the hind legs is shown by difficult action, the movement in standing giving an appearance of weakness, the legs seeming to drag and get in the way of each other. There is very little chance of cure, and attempts at such results are better left to the duly qualified veterinary surgeon; but the following known treatment will alleviate, and is at once the most merciful to the animal, and holds out the best hopes of at least partial recovery: Keep in a loose box well littered, and let the animal have perfect rest, regulate the bowels by soft food, roots and green-meat, and give tonics. Mayhew recommends half a grain of strychnine daily to be gradually increased to $1\frac{1}{2}$gr. in six weeks. The ball might be made as follows:

Ball for Paralysis.—Strychnine $\frac{1}{2}$gr., gentian powder $\frac{1}{2}$oz., made into a ball with treacle.

Keep the horse warm, especially across the loins, and friction with a rough brush or wisp may be useful if freely and frequently applied to the hind quarters.

Parrot mouth is that malformation which in dogs is termed "overshot" and "pig-jawed"—the upper incisors meeting no resistance from the under, grow long and overlap them, and this, as a matter of course, renders it difficult for the horse to pick up his corn, and causes him to waste a portion of it. There is no means of remedying the evil where it exists, but it could easily be bred out by careful selection, just as in bull terriers, where the first cross shows the protruding under jaw, the modern specimen has by selection been bred with a perfectly level mouth.

Pleurisy and Pneumonia, or Inflammation of the Lungs.—Modern veterinarians recognise pleurisy and pneumonia as distinct diseases—pleurisy being inflammation of the pleura or thin membrane which lines the thorax and envelopes the lungs, pneumonia applying to inflammation of the lungs; but the distinction is too fine to be of any practical use to those to whom these articles are addressed, as only the practised surgeon would be able to detect the difference, and the general treatment is the same. Inflammation of the lungs is a very common and a very dangerous disease, requiring prompt treatment on its first symptoms being observed. These are extreme dulness, unwillingness to move, laboured breathing, loss of appetite. As the disease proceeds the pulse increases, but lacks power, the flanks heave, the breathing becomes quicker and still more laboured, the ears hang listlessly, and these and the legs become cold, the coat gets rough, the eye shows red, and the lining membrane of the extended nostrils looks inflamed, the horse stands forward and wide in front, and wears an anxious and dejected look of pain. Any attempt he makes to lie down aggravates his state, giving evident pain. Costiveness is invariably an accompanying symptom.

The first step in combating the disease is to bleed freely from a large orifice till signs of faintness appear, when the orifice should at once be closed. The quantity necessary to be taken will often be as much as five or six quarts. The bowels should be at once relieved, to which end give clysters of soap and warm water or gruel, with oil, and give also a drench of castor oil or linseed oil.

Aconite is a medicine resorted to in these cases, but it is not a safe thing except in professional hands. The following may be given night and morning, or once a day, according to circumstances, until the symptoms have abated:

Ball for Pneumonia.—Nitre, 2dr.; powdered leaves of digitalis, ½dr.; powdered camphor, ½dr., made into a ball with common mass (p. 21). Or the concentrated fever mixture:

Concentrated Fever Mixture.—A good reliable and convenient form for fever mixture is made as follows: Take concentrated Mindererus spirit 4oz.; nitrate of potash 1oz.; tincture of belladonna 1dr.; sweet spirit of nitre 1oz.; water sufficient to make 16oz. Dose, in feverish affections, a wineglassful in a pint of gruel every four or six hours whilst fever continues.

The horse must be kept comfortable, let him have a loose box well padded with tan or other soft material, take off his shoes, frequently hand rub the legs, and draw the ears gently to create warmth. Keep the horse sufficiently warm with body cloths, but on no account in a hot stable; cool pure air is absolutely necessary to recovery; the hot and vitiated air of a close stable is poison in every breath to the patient; let the food consist solely of gruel, well made, and hay tea; when he begins to recover increase the food cautiously, or a relapse is certain, which generally proves fatal; add to the gruel scalded oats, or give them alone in small quantities frequently, six or eight times a day. One of the first symptoms of recovery is the horse lying down. On no account disturb him; rest is the best of restorers to exhausted nature. As recovery goes on gradually increase the feed, and in a little time tonics may be given. The causes of this disease are exposure to cold and wet, especially after a quick ride or drive, which causes a sudden check of the perspiration. It so often follows culpable heedlessness of the animal's claim on his master as to reflect on him the most severe censure. Broken wind is not an unfrequent sequel to this disease.

Pneumonia.—See *Pleurisy* and *Pneumonia*.

Poll Evil.—That this terrible source of agony to the poor horse has, happily, vastly diminished to a great extent we are willing to believe, through the more humane treatment to which our equine drudges are treated.

To describe the pain and agony the horse suffering from poll evil has patiently to endure is beyond my power; but let the reader imagine such a "sore grievance," as the older writers term it, to afflict himself with the terrible remedies necessary to its eradication, and he may have to blush for the inhumanity of man, that could either by want of that proper care which he owes to the domestic life in his keeping, or through indulgence of brutal passion, inflict such torture, for, be it remembered, this is a wholly preventible evil.

Poll evil consists in the formation of abscess on the top and back part of the head. It may first be discovered by the animal stretching his neck, and holding his head forward as if afraid to move, which in fact he is, as the pain arising from the injury he has received is great, and tempting as food in his manger may be, he makes but slow progress with it. At this stage, if the hand is applied gently to the poll, and pressure by degrees used, the existence of the disease will be proved by the horse evincing pain, and it may be prevented from going further by the application of a blister, the most appropriate to the case being an etherial and acetous tincture of cantharides applied with a brush daily until vesication has taken place; but, unfortunately, it is often tampered with, the remedies of impostors being often preferred to the advice of our scientific men; poultices and cold applications are not sufficiently active, and their use may only waste time and insure the evil it is desired to avert. When not stopped in its first stages, matter is formed, and as the injury is not merely external, nature has difficulty in finding an outlet, so that deep sinuses or canals are formed and must be cut into by the surgeon's knife, at the expense of exquisite pain to the sufferer; but this temporary pain, keen though it be, is preferable to continuous agony, therefore do not hesitate, but let the experienced surgeon exercise his profession, for such cases are beyond home treatment, and it would be the grossest cruelty to attempt it; above all, be warned against permitting ignorant horse doctors to torture the animal by pouring into the abscess strong caustics, boiling liquors, &c., which can only intensify the disease at a fearful cost of suffering. The cause of poll-evil is always an external injury, often a blow from a stick or butt end of a whip; and another cause is the stupid plan of building stables with low roof and joists, and doors so low in the lintel, the result being that the horse, having his attention arrested at a critical moment by any unusual sight or sudden sound, throws his head up, receiving a violent blow, which ends in poll-evil.

Prick of the Sole.—This accident occurs in shoeing, not always from carelessness, although awkward men and novices are the greatest delinquents. Whenever such a thing does happen it is the smith's duty to admit it, and indeed to acquaint the owner with the mischance. Of course if the nail is at once driven into the sensitive part of the foot the injury is made instantly apparent, but if its point only reach into the soft horn contiguous to the sensitive lamina it will not be discovered until the weight of the horse on it bends it into the sensitive part, causing lameness, pain, and often a discharge. The obvious duty is to have the shoe removed, and as one by one the nails are drawn examine each for any moisture and any offensive smell. The hole where the prick has been caused should be pared out, and a little tow inserted, steeped in a mixture of one part of pure carbolic acid and fifteen parts glycerine. If there is much heat and suppuration the foot should be placed frequently in a bucket of warm water, which will relieve greatly. See also *Foot, Prick of the*.

Profuse Staling.—See *Diabetes*.

Prurigo.—This is a cutaneous affection arising from the state of the blood. It often appears during the spring of the year, and is probably caused by constant diet of dry provender; and if the natural desire for green food is to some extent indulged, it will often disappear without the necessity of having recourse to any other means, and, as a preventive, there is nothing so good as occasional feeds of carrots during the winter months. Prurigo is altogether distinct from mange, for which it might be mistaken, as both diseases cause intolerable itching; but in prurigo the skin, even where the hair has been rubbed off, does not become thickened and wrinkled, nor does any discharge ooze from it. When prurigo is discovered, give the horse less hay, substituting grass or clover, and give a few mashes if the itching is very great; let the groom sponge the parts frequently with the following, which will allay the irritation:

Lotion for Prurigo.—Take twelve good sized poppy heads, crush them, and boil them slowly in three quarts of water down to two quarts, strain, and add 1oz. of carbonate of potash, 3dr. of pure (crystalized) carbolic acid, and 4oz. of methylated spirit of wine. The horse should also have, in stubborn cases, 1dr. of Fowler's solution of arsenic in water daily, immediately after being fed, and one of the following powders nightly sprinkled over his damped corn or mash:

Tonic Powder.—Pure sulphate of iron, in powder, 1dr.; powdered gentian ½oz., powdered liquorice 3dr.

Pumiced Feet often follows as a result of inflammation of the laminæ which secrete the hoof; the work having been interrupted, irregularity of the horny secretion is shown, and between the more solid hoof and the sensitive laminæ an imperfect spongy mass takes the place of the perfect horn, and being incapable of giving that support which is required, the coffin horn presses through it and bulges it out. The horse with a naturally weak hoof is most subject to pumiced feet, which may be caused by working on hard stoney roads and paved streets. In pumiced feet, the hoof shows irregularity of deposit, and is thin and brittle; and in such cases the best that can be done is to adopt palliative measures, and the principal of these is in the system of shoeing. "Stonehenge" recommends a wide but thin web shoe, covering so much more of the foot as to guard it against stones and other convex bodies. Wet should be avoided as much as possible, as it renders the hoof more brittle, and the existing difficulty in shoeing is great. The regular use of the hoof ointment, prescribed on page 15, will do much good, and the horse should not be taken out, in wet weather especially, without first having the hoof brushed over with it. Arising from the same causes as pumiced feet is seedy toe, which will be dealt with in its order. See also *Foot, Pumiced*.

Q.

Quittor is an excessively painful disease, and one the treatment of which should be handed over to a qualified veterinary surgeon. It arises from a suppurating corn, a prick in shoeing, or an internal injury produced by a tread or blow on the coronet, which has set up inflammation, and gone on to the destruction of healthy tissue and formation of pus or matter, which can find no way of escape through the hard substances of the coronet or the impervious hoof; and nature, in her endeavour to throw off this effete matter, makes sinuses or narrow channels in various directions to that end. The result generally is great swelling of the coronet, with extreme heat and intense pain, before the matter forces a way out. The pipes or sinuses should be opened up to give free discharge of the matter; but as some will be deep seated, quittor is not a disease fit for home treatment by the amateur, but should be entrusted to the professional man, who is thoroughly acquainted with the anatomy of the horse's foot, and accustomed to use the knife. If cases of lameness were not treated so lightly as they often are when first observed there would be fewer instances of quittor.

R.

Rheumatism.—Horses frequently suffer from rheumatism, sometimes in conjunction with influenza, but more often following that or some other serious disease. The sudden lameness and halting action of horses caused by rheumatism is often mistaken for strain or other injury, but the shifting nature of the former soon reveals the truth, as the horse with shoulder lameness one day may show the disease in the hip the next; it flies about from one leg to another. The secretion of synovia or joint oil is increased by it, and there is often considerable swelling of the limb, with a puffiness of the parts secreting joint oil. In acute rheumatism there is always more or less fever, and the severe pain the animal suffers is shown by his short jerky breathing, and the evident unwillingness to use the affected limb.

The remedies mostly relied on in rheumatism are outward applications, but in cases where fever exists a febrifuge drench or ball should be given. Colchicum or meadow saffron is a favourite remedy, and the most likely to prove successful; it may be given in doses of one to two drachms of the powdered corm combined with two drachms of powdered nitrate of potash. The smaller dose may be administered night and morning in a mash. There are numberless liniments and embrocations for the cure of rheumatism made which are all more or less useful. The best I believe to be the liniment of aconite, but it is a very powerful poison and dangerous in unskilled hands. One of the two following may be tried and will be likely to give relief and hasten the cure:

Liniments for Rheumatism.—(1) Take soap liniment 16oz., tincture of cantharides 1oz., laudanum 2oz., spirit of hartshorn 1oz., mixed; or (2) rape oil 4oz., oil of thyme 2oz., oil of cajeput 1oz., oil of turpentine 4oz., spirits of hartshorn 4oz., laudanum 1oz., mixed.

Whichever is used must be applied with considerable friction, and the rubbing kept up for some time. If the horse is fleshy and gross in body the bowels should be acted on by means of mashes and green food, withholding corn, but if he begins to lose flesh and strength give boiled or steamed oats, and old beans.

Ringbone.—This is a bony deposit just above the coronet, mostly occurring in heavy draught horses, and oftenest seen in the hind legs. The cause may be a blow, but generally speaking it is the result of the great stress on the parts, as the horse with a heavy load is pressed to the utmost of his strength in taking it up hill, when, as a consequence, inflammation is set up, and when that passes an osseous deposit takes place, which interferes with the natural free use of the foot, and thus detracting greatly from the value and usefulness of the animal. The only hope of cure is in the use of the firing iron, and repeated blistering, the best blister for the purpose being the red or biniodide of mercury (p. 24). At the same time the horse should have cooling medicine, as the firing sets up inflammation as the first process towards the absorption of the bony deposit. Give, therefore, after proper preparation, a dose of physic; let the horse have mashes, roots, and green meat, and 1oz. of nitre in a pail of water. The blister must be continued for some time, leaving it off for a few days when the part is too sore for its application, and again renewing it to keep up the irritation.

Ringworm.—Ringworm appears in bare circular patches quite denuded of hair, scurvy raised at the edge, and, if neglected, ulcerating there. It is not of very common occurrence, and should never be seen in a well regulated stable where cleanliness prevails, and the horses are properly groomed. It is somewhat difficult to eradicate, and the nostrums for its cure are numberless. The best cure is, I believe, the ointment of iodide of sulphur (p. 61), of the strength one part iodide to seven parts of simple ointment. The part affected should be well washed with soap and water, carefully dried, and the ointment well rubbed in night and morning. Among the other remedies we may mention iodide of lead, in form of ointment, saturated solution of sulphate of iron, creosote two parts, mixed with eight parts hogs' lard, and carbolic acid one part, glycerine nine parts. Mayhew recommends the following alterative and tonic drink to be given each night:

Alterative and Tonic Drink.—Fowler's solution of arsenic 2dr., tincture of muriate of iron 3dr., in half a pint of water.

This should be continued till all trace of the disease has disappeared.

Roaring.—This too common state of the horse is well known to all familiar with horses. The name is given to the unnatural sound emitted by the horse in breathing, and differs greatly in degree. It is an affection of the larynx or upper part of the windpipe, caused by thickening of the lining membrane, or from the tumours of strangles, chronic cough, or some other affection of the outer respiratory organs, and frequently from distortion of the larynx, from the head being kept in an unnatural position by the bearing rein. Preventive measures and those for the alleviation of the disease are alone worth considering, as there is no cure for roaring. All coughs and affections of the throat should receive prompt and careful attention, and the animal not too speedily put into work on recovery. The means for alleviation are the same as described for broken wind.

S.

Sallenders.—See *Mallenders and Sallenders*.

Seedy Toe.—This is a separation of the two layers of horny matter forming the hoof. These, the outer hard portion to which the shoe is nailed, and the inner soft and lighter portion are, in a healthy state, closely united, but from hard work, especially on the paved streets of towns, the secreting power which keeps up the connection becomes lost, the separation is apparent, and the treatment consists in paring away the outer or old horn, and giving the horse rest, in order that the new and inner layer may develop into the firm substance necessary for the support of the heavy weight of the horse and endure the rough contact with hard roads; a considerable period of rest should be given for this purpose as will be evident to anyone who considers the slow growth of a broken finger nail, even when no use of it interferes with the process.

Sitfast.—This is the name given to a hard callous lump or sore, generally caused by the friction of a badly fitting saddle, or the action on the same of an awkward rider; they are not unlike corns on the human foot, but frequently ulcerate round their edges. There are two modes of treatment—to cut them out and apply a lotion, such as chloride of zinc, 0.gr. to 4oz. of water; or, as most careful grooms would notice the sitfast before it came to ulceration, to apply a pad of tow or lint well saturated with vinegar and water, or what is better, the following cheap cooling lotion:

Cooling Lotion.—Sal ammoniac ½oz., acetic acid 2oz. (or vinegar half a pint), spirits of wine 2oz., water to make a quart.

If the constant application of this, with freedom from the saddle, which is absolutely necessary, fails to remove the sitfast, rub the hardened tissue with mild blistering ointment (pp. 12 and 17), which will generally dissipate the evil. In doing so, should the clys of the sitfast be in an uncertain state, the part where the skin is broken should be carefully guarded from contact with the blister.

Sore Throat.—This is recognised by the difficulty in swallowing, even water being in considerable proportion returned by the nostrils. The horse should be confined in a loose box, and liberally supplied with green food, steamed corn, and oatmeal gruel. These should be offered in small quantities at frequent intervals, and not left standing to get tainted by the breath of the horse, and the atmosphere of the stable. When very severe it becomes necessary to blister the throat, which can be done best with the cantharidine blistering ointment (pp. 12 and 17), or the following rubefacient liniment may answer the purpose without actual blistering:

Liniment for Sore Throat.—Take rape oil 2oz., spirit of hartshorn 2oz., spirit of turpentine 2oz., oil of origanum 1oz., tincture of cantharides 1oz.; mix and apply night and morning, rubbing well in with a piece of flannel.

The bowels should be kept free by soft food, instead of resorting to physic, and the following electuary will give great relief:

Electuary.—Take powdered opium 4dr., powdered catechu 2oz., powdered kino 2oz., powdered liquorice 4oz., honey or treacle ½lb.; mix very carefully, and place a dessert spoonful well back on the tongue three or four times a day.

The above may also be given with good effect in all cases of cough.

Spavin.—Spavin is a bony growth occurring on the inside of the hock, varying considerably in size, but always more or less considerably interfering with the action of the horse, although it does not in every case cause actual lameness; it is commonly said that cow-hocked horses are most liable to it, but this is doubtful, and it is rather in the light-boned weak-jointed specimens that it is to be expected. When spavin does not interfere with the usefulness of the horse it is better left alone than to submit the animal to torture with problematical results, and frequently perfect rest will be of great service. When remedial measures are adopted, the firing iron is generally depended on, its action followed up by the application of blisters, the best form being the red or biniodide of mercury (p. 24), of the strength of one part of the biniodide to seven parts of simple ointment. This has to be continuously applied, the object being to cause absorption of the bony deposit, which is a slow process.

Splent or Splint.—Splints or splents, as they are indifferently termed, are bony excrescences occurring on the inside of the knee of the foreleg, at its lower extremity, or on the inner side of the shank bone of either fore or hind leg, but mostly restricted to the fore leg. They vary in size, and can always be detected by an experienced person by passing the hand down the leg. The cause of them is inflammatory excitement of the membrane lining the bone, which produces a deposit of bone of unnatural growth. During its growth there will be tenderness, with more or less lameness, and where the deposit of bone is so placed that the muscles in use in the horse's movement of his leg pass over it, it is certain to cause pronounced lameness, but otherwise, although slightly unsightly, they do no harm, and frequently in the course of time disappear. They are found on young unbroken horses, as well as on such as have been worked. When they do not cause lameness or interfere with the action of a tendon the wisest plan is to leave them alone, as the only hopeful treatment is by setting up local inflammation, which is not always easy of control. When the splent interferes with the action of a tendon it should be dealt with by a practical veterinary surgeon. If any attempt is made to reduce the splent, one of the preparations of iodine will be the most reliable; the red iodide of mercury referred to in treating of spavin is the most active, or the iodide of lead, a dense powder of a yellow colour, much milder in its action, may be tried; it is used in form of ointment of the strength one part of iodide to seven parts of lard or simple ointment.

Stomach, Inflammation of.—See *Gastritis*.

Staggers—Stomach Staggers—Sleepy Staggers—Mad Staggers.—The two last terms refer to and are descriptive of two forms and stages of the same disease. This always arises from over gorging, and is especially apt to be produced if the horse has been kept long without food, the system temporarily exhausted by toil, and then a full meal of corn given, when from overtiredness the digestive organs fail to perform their functions. The symptoms of the sleepy stage are partly expressed in the term, and there is sonorous breathing, the head is dropped helplessly on the manger or pressed against the wall, there is constipation and scanty urine, and if the horse rouses from this state great thirst is evinced. Should water be allowed it swells the corn in the stomach, distending it, and causing inflammation, and the mad stage is quickly developed; but the sleepy stage may be quitted without this when the eye, hitherto dull, shows an unnatural brightness, the breathing becomes quick and short, and the animal displays great excitement and violence. Both of these forms or stages of the disease show the brain to be implicated. It is generally a fatal disease, against which there is the consolation that in almost if not every case it is preventible. The first endeavour should be to relieve the overloaded stomach, which is the primary cause of all the symptoms; for this purpose powerful doses of purgatives are given in solution, together with the administration of clysters, which should be thrown up every ten or fifteen minutes. The former may consist of the following:

Purge for Staggers.—4dr. to 6dr. of aloes, dissolved in half a pint of water, and with ½oz. of carbonate of soda, and 1oz. of brandy or other spirit, or of sweet spirit of nitre, or sal volatile if at hand.

Mayhew objects to the administration of watery purgatives, because they swell the corn in the stomach, and prescribes oil in quart doses, followed in six hours by a second quart, with 20 drops of croton oil added, and in six hours more, if no improvement has taken place, another quart with 30 drops of croton oil. The best oil to use is raw linseed oil. The clyster may be made as follows:

Clyster.—Spirit of turpentine 6oz.; castor oil half a pint; oatmeal gruel 3 quarts.

In bad cases of staggers no treatment is of any avail, and in all cases it is much the best plan to place the case in the hands of a qualified veterinary surgeon, but the treatment prescribed may be adopted where such services are difficult to obtain, or pending the arrival of the surgeon.

Staling, Profuse.—See *Diabetes*.

Strangles.—This is a disease incident to young horses, generally happening between the ages of two and five years, and very often appearing soon after they are taken up from grass; the reason apparently for the latter fact being found in the too sudden change of diet from the soft natural grasses and succulent herbs to hard corn and dry hay, and no less by the equally great change from the open air to close stables, too often far from clean, and rarely with the slightest pretentions to ventilation, for it is too plain to all who choose to consider the subject, that those cases are rare where sanitary laws are properly considered and acted on in housing stock, but those who wish to see their young horses "safe through the strangles," will find their profit in a careful attention to such matters. Never, then, change a young horse's diet too suddenly, nor take him from the fields to be cooped up in a low-roofed unventilated and hot stable; cleanliness can always be observed and proper ventilation insured by a little trouble and outlay. Although this may not prevent the strangles, it helps to keep the horse in a better state to meet and master the disease, and renders dangerous forms of it less likely to occur. The disease is a febrile one, accompanied with general sickness and loss of appetite; then follows stiffness of the neck, with heat and tumefaction or swelling about the jaws, which is at first hard and hot to the touch; there is also a running at the nose, the swelling in the throat increases and goes on, the throat is sore, as shown in the act of swallowing, and the breathing is affected, until the swelling becomes a tumour, which, ripening and coming to a head between the jaws, is cut open or bursts, and discharges matter copiously, after which, with proper treatment, all danger is over. The fear is—and to prevent it requires constant watchfulness—that the tumour pressing against the windpipe might cause strangulation. The treatment to be adopted is first to provide suitable accommodation. A roomy box, shed, or other place well ventilated, and the horse well bedded; keep the strength up by giving such food in small quantities and at frequent intervals as will tempt him to eat; it must at same time be light and laxative whilst nourishing, such as corn bruised and steamed with carrots; a little mash of ground malt, good gruel made with hay tea, clover, and other available green food, but always given in small lots, not pitched before the horse, or he will soil it by breathing on it and pulling it about, and of course afterwards refuse it. The above mode of feeding will obviate the necessity of giving purging medicines; and bleeding should not be practised in strangles, as it weakens the system and prolongs the course of the disease and recovery from it. An important object is to forward the formation and ripening of the tumour, and this is done by the application of blisters in a fluid or semi-fluid form, for which the following recipe will be available:

Fluid Blisters.—Oil of cantharides (which is made by macerating or digesting one part of cantharides in eight parts of olive oil in a sand bath for two hours and then filtering) 6oz., strong mercurial ointment 2oz., mixed and rubbed well into the throat and swollen parts with the hand.

This will make the skin sore, and cause a slight discharge from it, but it will bring the tumour to a head, when it should be cut into, and the imprisoned matter let loose, and the parts should be pressed to get rid of it all, and afterwards kept strictly clean. I should have stated that after the application of the blister the part should be well fomented half a dozen times a day, with flannels wrung out of hot water, and a few folds of good thick flannel saturated with very warm water, carefully bound on by tying pieces of tape sewed to it, two from each side in front, and two just behind the ears. The suppuration should be encouraged at first by fomentations, and the strength of the horse kept up by a generous diet, and as the appetite increases, which it will with the relief felt from the discharge from the swellings, a few of the tonic powders (pp. 6, 21, and 53) should be given.

The dangers attending strangles are the fear of the horse being choked by the swelling before it is opened, to avoid which in an emergency the veterinary surgeon would open the windpipe. There is also the danger of relapse, when cure is always tardy; abscesses may form on various parts of the body, and complications take place which the veterinarian alone will be able to deal with. But the foregoing treatment carefully carried out will, except in rare cases, ensure against such untoward results.

Stringhalt.—This is the name given to the involuntary rapid jerking upward movement of the hind legs shown by some horses when starting. It is very easily recognised; horses afflicted with it always showing it when first brought out of the stable and after standing for some time; but it disappears when the animal is fairly in action. There is no cure for it that I am aware of.

Surfeit.—The disease known as surfeit consists, as far as its outward appearance goes, of a quantity of small round bumps which suddenly make their appearance on the skin, particularly of the neck, shoulders, and sides, and it is very similar to "heat lumps" that occasionally appear on the skin of man; it is generally caused by exposure to sudden changes of temperature, and very often from drinking cold water freely when the animal is warm. As a rule, the disease is easily managed, and does not last long, and will yield to a mild dose or two of laxative medicine, with change of diet, good nursing, and cooling alterative powders made of sulphur, antimony, and nitre, with some of the bitter and carminative seeds, a recipe for which has already been given (p. 50); in more severe cases, which are more likely to occur in horses that have been badly treated, the lumps, instead of disappearing, break and discharge from the centre, forming a scab, which ultimately comes off, bringing a portion of the hair with it. In such cases these spots should be frequently wetted with the following lotion:

Lotion for Surfeit.—Carbolic acid and glycerine (British Pharmacopœia) 1½oz., laudanum 2oz., carbonate of potash—commonly called salts of tartar—½oz., soft water 1 quart.

And, in addition to the powders prescribed above, give the following once a day:

Fowler's solution of arsenic 2 drachms, tincture of gentian 1oz., mixed in half a pint of water, and sprinkled over the corn and cut chaff.

If the horse is on dry food substitute for a portion of the hay cut grass or other green food, with a few carrots, if obtainable, and give a mash occasionally to keep the bowels in a laxative state. In no case should bleeding be resorted to for surfeit, except under the express direction of a veterinarian; and in the case of horses of weak constitution the severe attacks should be met by perfect rest in a roomy comfortable stable, and nourishing food supplied, giving no more medicine than will merely ensure the bowels being kept free.

Swollen or Filled Legs.—This is one of the troubles of the stable, to which heavy horses and those of a soft constitution are most liable. It generally appears in the luxuriously fed animal, after a rest day, and in such cases it would probably be avoided by judicious and quiet exercise. In cases where there is debility the animal should have a roomy box, good food, the tonic powders, and after fomenting the legs with hot water they should be thoroughly well hand rubbed, using the stimulating liniment (p. 24).

T.

Teeth, Caries and Irregularities of.—Caries, or decayed tooth, is occasionally met with in the horse, and when discovered it should be removed. Irregularities occur through the motion of the jaws, which is from side to side, wearing away one side of the grinders, leaving the other sharp and irregular, often so as to wound the tongue and cheeks in mastication, the pain produced throwing the horse off his feed, and preventing him chewing his food properly, instead of which, after rolling it into a ball, he ejects it, which is known as "quidding." As in this state of things the horse suffers pain and misery, and also quickly loses flesh and condition, the assistance of the veterinary surgeon should be sought, who, with instruments properly adapted to the purpose, will remove any diseased tooth, and cut down and file those requiring it. Care should be taken by those who feed horses that the corn is free from small stones and other hard substances which may accidentally find their way into it, as one such article might easily start permanent disease.

Another thing to be carefully looked after by horse owners is the too common custom of attendants giving medicines of various kinds surreptitiously; for although they may be actuated by good motives, and a laudable pride to see the animals under their charge excel their neighbour's in health and appearance, their ignorance leads them into serious and indeed dangerous mistakes; and not infrequently strong corrosive acids are administered, directly destructive to the teeth as well as the general health.

Teething.—During teething horses suffer from slight febrile affections, which, generally speaking, require no further treatment than a laxative, cooling diet, green food, with the corn steamed, and, if necessary, a mild purging ball.

Thrush, or "frush," as it is called by some stablemen, generally occurs in the hind feet; it is a disease of an inflammatory nature in its earliest stage, going on to suppuration, the parts affected being the sensible frog, which becomes ulcerous and discharges from the cleft a very fœtid matter of a peculiarly abhorrent smell, the soft horn adjacent to and protecting the sensible frog becomes rotten and ragged, and must be cleared away with the knife to make the real seat of the disease accessible to curative agents. The best of these are the following:

Lotion for Thrush.—Pure carbolic acid ½oz., glycerine 3oz., rectified spirits of wine 2dr., mixed, to be applied to the ulcerous parts between the clefts of the frog by means of tow tied on the end of a stick; or instead of the above, chloride of zinc ½dr., distilled water 8oz., mixed, used as above. Both of these destroy the fœtor of the discharge, or the ointment recommended for canker (p. 25) may be used with good result.

Thrush is almost a wholly preventable disease, although it is sometimes the result of inflammation and contraction of the feet, in which cases it generally appears in the fore ones; it is also produced in all four feet by long exposure to wet, as in horses pastured in soft, marshy meadows, but it is oftenest met with in the hind feet only, and caused by want of proper attention and cleanliness in the stable. When the dung and litter are allowed to accumulate, it collects and holds the urine like a sponge, and this fermenting acrid filth is absorbed by the frog, producing the ulceration described. Where such a state of things exists the first step to a cure is of course its removal. Let the stable be well cleansed and disinfected, see that the drains are open, supply the horse with a clean dry bed, and avoid the accumulation of saturated litter. Thrush, in its incipient stage, before the discharge takes place, is a frequent cause of stumbling, the frog being tender, pressure on a stone causes sudden pain, and the animal is apt to go on his knees before he can recover himself.

Tympanitis.—See *Colic.*

V.

Vein, Inflammation of.—This is of a dangerous nature, ending fatally in form of phrenitis; it is of comparatively rare occurrence, since the absurd system of periodic spring and autumn bleeding of horses has been given up. It occurs when horses, having been bled from the neck vein, are allowed to graze or eat from the floor, and permitted free motion. The lips of the orifice made by the fleam separate, a small lump forms, which ultimately discharges matter, and similar lumps appear along the vein following the same course. The treatment consists in repeated blistering, whilst the horse should be fed with nutritious but soft food; such cases should however be left to the skill of the veterinary surgeon.

W.

Warts.—Most people are familiar with the excrescences on the skin known by this name. There are several kinds which appear on the horse, but the difference between them would not be recognised by the amateur, and the treatment is in all cases the same, either they should be removed by the knife when they are solitary—and this method can be adopted—or caustics should be regularly applied until they are burnt off; of these the best is the lunar caustic, or nitrate of silver, and the glacial acetic acid. In using the latter care must be taken that it does not spread over the sound skin, which it is apt to do, being very thin. It is easiest applied with a camel's hair pencil. When warts appear they should be at once attacked, as although they do not, according to an exploded superstition, "breed" in the sense that animals or vegetables do, yet it is satisfactorily shown by experience that when allowed to remain the disposition to develop them is increased, and when they are removed this is discouraged and stopped. It seems almost needless to say that the various plans adopted to "charm" away these excrescences is a silly superstition. Yet I have met many simple people with a firm belief in such nonsense.

Warbles or **Warblets** are small lumps caused by the heat and friction of the saddle, which, if care be not taken, become tumours; generally they disappear if the saddle is altered to give relief from pressure on the part, and when that fails the horse should be thrown off work and the warbles rubbed with blistering ointment (p. 24).

Windy Colic.—See *Colic*.

Windgalls are small round or oval puffy swellings above the fetlock, brought on by severe work, which cause irritation of the sacs containing the synovia or joint oil, which lubricates the tendons, so that more of it is secreted than is required for that purpose, or than the sacs can contain; hence windgalls are seen most prominently after a hard day, although on the other hand they sometimes disappear after a hard run, when a puffiness of the whole leg, from fetlock to hock, appears.

The treatment for windgalls consists of cold fomentations with bandages, and pressure by means of pads. The cooling lotion already given (p. 37) is an excellent preparation for this purpose, or blisters may be applied, in which case biniodide of mercury blister (p. 24) will answer best, and where this is used the horse should have a physic ball (pp. 37 and 73) and have mashes and a portion of green food or roots, and three days after the physic 1oz. of nitre.

Withers (Fistulous).—See *Fistulous Withers.*

Worms.—There are several kinds of these parasites that infest the horse, and their presence is not easy to determine, unless actually seen, and the symptoms and consequences of other diseases are not unfrequently attributed to worms. Bots, which although generally spoken of as worms, are totally different from those under present consideration, so I have treated them separately under that head. The varieties of worms which horses are subject to are the tape worm, a long, flat, jointed worm, occurring very rarely, and that generally in young, half starved animals. It is difficult to eradicate, as each joint is capable of reproduction, so that when it is known to exist, repeated doses of vermifuges, as worm-expelling medicines are called, must be given, and the excrements should be watched and burned or deeply buried. Turpentine is one of the best medicines for the destruction of this parasite. The dose of it is for a foal from 3 to 6 months old, ½oz. to 1oz.; from 1 to 2 years, 2oz.; over that age, from 3oz. to 4oz. It should be given in the form of an emulsion, that is beat up with white of eggs or mucilage of acacia, and mixed with ale, stout, or oil, or it may be given mixed with raw linseed oil alone, from a pint to a quart. If the spirit of turpentine alone proves ineffectual in their removal, slightly lessen the dose, and incorporate with it from ½drm. to 1¼drm. of ethereal extract of male fern, commonly called oil of male fern.

THE LONG ROUND WORM, called the *lumbricus*, or *Ascaris lumbricoides*, measures from 6in. to 12in. in length, some specimens even more than that; they are round, and pointed at each end; they often exist in large numbers, and keep the animals they infest lean and ragged looking by absorbing the food intended for the support of the horse. For these turpentine may also be given in linseed oil or according to the following formula :—

Worm Mixture: Spirit of turpentine two ounces; essential oil of wormwood, twenty drops; linseed oil, half a pint; infusion of quassia, half a pint, to which has been added one drachm of salts of tartar, after which mix with the oil and turpentine, shake well together, and give for a dose; or the following may be given:

Worm Ball: Tartar emetic, 1½ drachms; powdered ginger, 1 drachm; Barbadoes aloes, 4 drachms; soap, 1 drachm, made into one ball, one to be given every alternate morning before feeding the horse till four have been given. Some practitioners give the tartar emetic alone in the morning, fasting. From one to two drachms each morning in this way for six days, followed by a strong physic ball on the seventh day. Calomel is also administered as a vermifuge, given overnight in doses of one to two drachms, and followed in the morning by a physic ball.

NEEDLE OR THREAD WORMS are the smallest of these intestinal parasites; they occupy the large intestines, the colon, and rectum, and create great irritation, and cause the horse great annoyance by the itching they produce, so that he will rub his buttocks and tail against walls and posts till hair and skin are both rubbed off. This constant rubbing of the hind quarters is a sure sign of worms, and the presence of these pests is also generally indicated by the adhesion of yellow mucous-like matter about the anus, or a dry yellow powder about the anus and between the thighs. It is very difficult to reach these parasites by medicine through the stomach, although all the medicines named above are used for their expulsion. Injections are, however, often more effectual. A quantity of train oil may be thrown up, or instead a weak solution of aloes, or of common salt a dessert spoonful in a quart of water. There is also an instrument in use by which an enema of tobacco smoke can be administered, and that proves often very effectual, bringing the worms away dead with the next motion of the bowels.

There are numerous other remedies for worms, some of them very dangerous, and should never be given except under the direction of a veterinary surgeon. Such are arsenic, savin, and tobacco. Familiarity we know breeds contempt, and the ostler or carter who smokes and chews tobacco may think he cannot injure a horse with it; but such is not the case. Calomel and tartar emetic must also be used cautiously. Of other vermifuges that have been recommended for the horse I may name cowhage, powdered glass, and granulated tin, which act mechanically, also kousoo, areca nut, empyreumatic oils, consisting of ammonia, creosote, acetic acid, &c.; but perhaps the best and safest treatment is oleaginous purges with clysters, or the turpentine, male fern, and wormwood emulsions.

Horses suffering much from worms generally look ragged and poor; the coat is harsh and staring, and there is often so much itching that the horse will bite himself and pull the hair off in parts. After the expulsion of the worms the horse should be generously fed, and should also have a course of the tonic powders (pp. 6, 21, 53, and 70) which I have elsewhere recommended to improve the appetite, assist digestion, and strengthen the constitution.

Wounds.—Wounds are of various kinds, and the horse, unfortunately, is very liable to them, although they often occur through no fault of his own. They differ widely in their severity and the danger attending them. It is only slight superficial wounds that can be safely treated by the non-professional, and whether the wound is of such a nature may generally be determined by a careful examination, which should always be conducted with the utmost quietness, so as not to excite the already alarmed horse. In slight hurts, clean by sponging water (blood warm), and afterwards apply compound tincture of aloes or Friar's Balsam, with a soft brush or feather; but in all deep or doubtful wounds it is wisest to consult a veterinary surgeon, as no one without a sound knowledge of the anatomy of the horse can safely be trusted with such cases.

DRUGS USED IN HORSE DISEASES, THEIR MEDICINAL QUALITIES, DOSES, &c.

To enumerate and characterise all the drugs used for the horse in veterinary practice would require much more space than is at our present command, and after all might prove more confusing than useful to those for whom I write. These medicinal substances are arranged into groups according to their prophylactic, or preservative and therapeutic or curative properties, such, for instance, as cathartics, purgatives, and aperients, all of which act on the system so as to cause an increased discharge of faeces, and include a great number of substances, as aloes, olive oil, castor oil, croton oil, calomel, &c., and astringents, which, given internally, have an opposite effect, checking purgation, and when applied externally diminish discharges from wounds, such as alum, catechu, preparations of zinc, nutgalls, &c. I have therefore selected those of each class in highest repute, and most likely to be of practical use to those who consult these pages, and for convenience follow up the alphabetical order adopted in treating of the diseases for which these drugs are used as remedies.

Acetic Acid.—This drug is the same in character as common vinegar, but it is seven times stronger; and as vinegar is kept in every house, I would not have noticed acetic acid, only that it enters into the composition of the Concentrated Cooling Lotion, which I recommend to be kept at hand ready for use in any sudden emergency: it is also used as a solvent for camphor and other essential oils, in which combination it is used as a rubefacient—that is, to create redness of the skin without actually blistering—and cantharides digested in it in its diluted form, that is, of the same strength of vinegar is used as a blister. Recipe for *Concentrated Cooling Lotion*: Take muriate of ammonia (sal ammoniac) 2 ounces, boiling water 1 pint, strong acetic acid 4 ounces, methylated spirit of wine 1oz.; mix, and before using the lotion dilute it with eight times its bulk of cold water: it is used for reducing local inflammation, such as occurs in bruises, sprains, &c.

Acetate of Lead.—See *Lead*.
Acetate of Zinc.—See *Zinc*.
Acids used as Caustics.—See *Caustics*.
Allspice or Pimento.—This is a stimulant and tonic often used in compounding what are so widely known as "condition powders." Half an ounce may be given to improve the appetite, once a day, mixed with the corn and cut chaff. For this purpose, of course, the ground pimento berries must be used; and in this and all cases where dry powders are given with the corn it should be first damped and the powder shaken over it and evenly mixed.

Aloes is a purgative, and, as such, one of the most important drugs in veterinary practice. There are several kinds of it; that preferred as most suitable for the horse is the Barbadoes aloes; it is generally given in form of a ball, the dose ranging from four to seven drachms. Physic balls of various strength can be purchased at most chemists, and, as a rule, may be depended on; but some tradesmen for a little extra profit substitute common and cheaper kinds, less suitable, adding croton oil to insure purgation, than which, practically, nothing can be more dishonest if a simple aloetic ball is required. The following form for a five drachm physic ball, which is a very common dose for a horse, will be useful to those who wish to prepare it themselves: *Physic Ball*: Take 5½ drachms of Barbadoes aloes, break small and melt in a cup or small gallipot; add 2 drachms of good powdered ginger and a teaspoonful of glycerine, and make the whole firm by working into it a little linseed meal; roll it into the proper shape, and keep in a cool place, it will remain of a proper consistence for a long time.

In giving a horse a physic ball, it is very important to prepare him for it by giving bran or bran and linseed mashes beforehand—indeed, the horse should have nothing else for twenty-four hours before the ball is given. Aloes is also used for applying to wounds that it is desirable to heal, cuts, bruises where the skin is broken, sore shoulders, &c., a little of the powder may be sprinkled on, or, what is better, a little of the following applied with a feather: *Compound Tincture of Aloes*: Aloes, 2 ounces; gum myrrh 1 ounce; gum benjamin, 1 ounce; methylated or rectified spirit of wine, 1 pint; water, ½ pint. The gums must be broken small, put into a quart bottle, the spirit and water added, and the contents frequently shaken. Of course a fourth or eighth part only may be made. It is very useful, and should be kept in the stable.

Alteratives.—Alterative medicines are those which slowly and imperceptibly, by often repeated doses long continued, cause a change in the state of the body. The term is a very popular one; but it is doubtful whether the majority of those who use it have a very clear or definite notion of what they mean. The word appears to have a sort of charm, for stablemen and others, who generally possess a famous recipe, which is referred to with a mixture of pride and mystery as possessing wonderful powers of "cleansing the blood," "clearing away all gross and foul humours," and, in fact, working such miracles of good by some occult process as to put poor nature to the blush. Some of these compounds would be most deleterious, and, indeed, absolutely dangerous, but for the fact that the chemist who dispenses them uses his own judgment as to the ingredients he puts in. As long as these consist merely of a little sulphur, crude antimony, and aromatic seeds, they do no harm, but the use of powerful alteratives, such as arsenic, mercurial preparations, &c., is highly reprehensible in unskilled hands.

The following is a fair sample of what is usually called "alterative," "condition," and "coating" powders, and, as I have excluded all such active but very dangerous drugs as arsenic, cantharides, &c., they may be given with advantage when the horse is "off his feed," or in any way "out of sorts." *Alterative and Condition Powders:* Take powdered nitre, flowers of sulphur, and black antimony, of each 4oz.; powdered gentian root, ½lb.; powdered liquorice, 4oz.; powdered carraways, ¼lb.; powdered aniseed, ½lb.; and powdered cumin seeds and coriander seeds each ¼lb.; well mixed together, and one to two tablespoonfuls given sprinkled on the corn and cut chaff every night.

Alum.—This common and generally known article is an astringent, and as such is given in diarrhœa, and also in cases of diabetes or profuse staling. The dose is from ¼oz. to ½oz.; it is also useful as an external application. The following ointment is often of advantage in grease: *Ointment for Grease:* Finely powdered alum, ½ oz.; rosin ointment, 1 oz., mixed.

Ammonia.—This is at the ordinary temperature of the air gaseous, but in solution in water, and several of its combinations, it is largely used in horse medicine. *Liquid ammonia*—popularly known as *spirits of hartshorn*—is given in windy colic in doses of ½oz. to 1oz., in not less than a pint and a half of water, ale, or gruel; but for this purpose the aromatic spirit of ammonia is generally preferred, and the spirit of hartshorn is mostly used in form of liniment for sprains, bruises, &c., for which the following is a useful and cheap form: *Liniment for Sprains:* Spirit of hartshorn, spirit of turpentine, and rape oil, equal parts mixed.

AROMATIC SPIRIT OF AMMONIA, popularly known as spirit of sal volatile, is also largely used in veterinary practice. It is a stimulant and anti-spasmodic, and proves of great use in gripes, as it dispels flatulence, and also stimulates the stomach. The dose is 1oz. to 2oz. in at least a pint and a half of water, gruel, or other simple liquid. The following combination of it makes a good preparation for fret, colic, or gripes: *Gripe Tincture:* Spirit of sal volatile, 6oz.; sweet spirit of nitre, 6oz.; essential oil of peppermint, ½oz.; essential oil of pimento, ½oz.; laudanum, 5oz.; and essence of ginger, 2oz.; mixed. Dose: One to two wineglassfuls in a quart of gruel; this should be kept in a glass stoppered bottle.

HYDROCHLORATE OF AMMONIA, known as sal ammoniac, is very useful as an ingredient in cooling lotions for applications to swellings and inflamed parts where the skin is not broken. A bottle of the following should be kept in the stable medicine chest or somewhere handy in a cool place, as when wanted it will generally be in a hurry. *Concentrated Cooling Lotion:* Take sal ammoniac in powder 4oz., boiling water half a pint, gradually add the water to the sal ammoniac in a mortar, rubbing it to dissolve as much as possible, pouring the solution into a bottle, then take strong acetic acid half a pint and in the same way treat the undissolved sal ammoniac with it and mix with the watery solution, and add to the whole 4oz. of methylated spirit of wine. When used it must be mixed in the proportions of one cupful of lotion to seven to ten cupfuls of cold water.

SOLUTION OF ACETATE OF AMMONIA, or Mindererus's Spirit, is a combination of ammonia with acetic acid, and is a febrifuge or fever medicine. It is generally combined with nitrate or chlorate of potash, and sweet spirit of nitre. The following is a useful form of it to keep at hand, and in a well-corked bottle, and in a cool place, it will keep good for years:— *Concentrated fever mixture*: Nitrate of potash, 1oz.; water, 8oz. Dissolve the nitrate of potash and add the concentrated Mindererus's spirit, 4oz.; sweet spirit of nitre, 3oz. The dose is two tablespoonfuls, diluted with a pint of water or gruel, and it may with perfect safety be given in colds, influenza, &c., twice or thrice a day, but it is generally better in these cases to give a purge first.

Animal Oil, also known as Dippel's oil, an abominable compound of common oil, paraffin, acetic acid, &c., is now obsolete.

Antimony.—There are three preparations of antimony to which I must refer, and as being much the best known among horsemen, I will take first the black or crude antimony, and I may observe here that liver of antimony is the same thing, as far as its medicinal properties go, and, indeed, often literally so, being merely the black antimony with a little Armenian bole, or red earth added. Crude antimony is considered to be an alterative, and as such is given in doses of from a quarter to half an ounce, generally mixed with nitre and aromatic seeds, and in the form I have given under "Alteratives" it can do no harm, but the profession discard it, and when they use antimony do so in the more active and reliable form of tartarised antimony or tartar emetic.

BUTTER OF ANTIMONY, is a well known yellowish red liquid, a mild caustic, used as an application in cases of canker, corns, &c. It must not be mixed with water, as that decomposes it, rendering it useless.

TARTARISED ANTIMONY, OR TARTAR EMETIC, is a preparation of power, and must be used with caution. It is given to reduce feverishness, in doses of half a drachm to a drachm. The following powder may, in such cases, be given twice a day:—Tartar emetic, ½dr.; powdered camphor, 1dr.: nitre, 2dr.; powdered liquorice, ½oz.; to be given in a mash, or, if refused, made into a ball, and so administered.

Aqua Fortis.—See *Nitric Acid*.

Arnica.—Arnica has for a long time been popular as a cure for swellings, lameness, &c. It is used in the form of tincture, made by macerating the root or leaves or both in spirit, and applied as a lotion diluted with water—one part of tincture to ten or twelve parts of water.

Balsam of Sulphur.—See *Oil of Sulphur*.

Belladonna, or Deadly Nightshade.—The extract of this plant is used, but it is of too dangerous a nature to be prescribed by any except professional men. The following prescription is from a veterinary surgeon of eminence; I have often prepared and known great relief afforded by it to horses suffering from broken wind, roaring, whistling, and other affections of the respiratory organs:—Take extract of belladonna, ½dr.; powdered camphor, ½dr.; powdered squills, 2dr.; gum arabic, 1dr.; and common mass, ½oz., made into a ball; one to be given daily. The balls should be first wrapped in a piece of tissue paper, and then in a piece of tinfoil, to prevent the camphor from evaporating. Of course, the tinfoil must be taken off before the ball is given.

Bichloride of Mercury.—See *Mercury*.
Blue Stone, or Blue Vitriol.—See *Copper*.
Brimstone.—See *Sulphur*.
Calamine.—See *Zinc*.
Calomel.—This is a subchloride of mercury, a very powerful drug, and one used with little discretion by the common horse doctors who still exercise too much power in this country. It is a most useful drug, but, in the hands of the untrained, a dangerous one. It is often added with good effects to aloetic purges, especially where the liver is to be acted on. It is also given in inflammation of the bowels and in dysentery, in combination with opium. The dose is one to two drachms. It is greatly extolled as a vermifuge, but there are safer expellents of worms, indeed, these parasites are comparatively rare in the horse, and bots no medicine can reach or affect.

Camphor.—Camphor is a narcotic; but it is more used externally in the form of liniments for sprains, bruises, &c., combined with spirits, ammonia, soap, or fixed oils.

Cantharides—Spanish Fly or Blistering Fly.—The principal use of these insects is as a blister, and the forms in which they are so used I have noticed under "Blisters" (p. 11). However valuable cantharides may be as an internal medicine, they should not be given except under professional advice or supervision, and the use of them in so called condition powders, or in any way by unprofessional persons, cannot be too strongly condemned.

Carbonate of Soda.—See *Soda*.

Carraways.—Most people are familiar with carraway seeds, as they are used so largely as a culinary spice. In horse medicine they are useful from their aromatic odour and agreeable flavour, as an addition to more active medicines, and are in themselves carminative, stomachic, and stimulating. They answer all the purposes of such other seeds and spices as aniseed, coriander, cumin, fenugreek, pimento, &c.; but in popular recipes for horse powders and cattle drenches, cattle food, &c., a number of these are generally combined.

Castor Oil is a purgative, but is seldom given to the horse, linseed-oil being both better and cheaper.

Caustic, Lunar.—See *Silver, Nitrate of*.
Chloride of Sodium.—See *Sodium*.
Chloride of Zinc.—See *Zinc*.
Chloroform.—For professional use only, being dangerous in unskilled hands.

Copper.—Two preparations of copper may be referred to here—the diacetate, known as verdigris, and the sulphate or blue stone.

DIACETATE OF COPPER is used to stimulate foul ulcerous sores, that are termed indolent or slow to heal, in the form of liniment of verdigris, better known by the name of *Egyptiacum*, for the making of which there are several forms; but if required it is better to purchase it from the chemist than attempt to make it; it consists of verdigris, alum or vinegar, and honey or treacle boi'ed together.

SULPHATE OF COPPER, BLUE STONE, OR BLUE VITRIOL, OR BLUE COPPERAS, for by all these names is it known, is a valuable preparation, and is applied externally for the same purposes as verdigris; it is applied to indolent sores and to proud flesh on sores, either by rubbing with the smooth side of a large crystal or dusting on a little in a state of fine powder, and it is a principal ingredient in a majority of advertised remedies for canker in the foot as also for "the foul" in cattle, and foot rot in sheep. An excellent form of ointment for these purposes is given under "Canker." Sulphate of copper is also administered in Farcy and Glanders, as is also the diniodide, another preparation of copper. As a tonic it is given in doses of one to two drachms, in a ball, as follows : Pure sulphate of copper 1½oz., ground ginger 3oz., ground gentian 3oz., common mass 6oz., carefully mixed and divided into twelve balls, one to be given twice a day after the horse has been fed.

Corrosive Sublimate.—See *Mercury*.

Croton Oil.—This is another fixed oil, made from the seeds of *Croton tiglium*, an Indian plant. It is a most powerful drastic purgative, and should not be given except under professional advice. The dose for the horse is twenty to thirty drops. Croton cake, which is the crushed seeds after the oil has been expressed from them, has also been used, but it must of necessity be of uncertain strength, which is a source of danger.

Deadly Nightshade.—See *Belladonna*.

Digitalis or Foxglove.—This plant is well known to nearly every one. The leaves, dried and powdered, are a very valuable horse medicine, but even professional men use it with caution, and it should never be given by anyone else.

Dippel's Oil.—See *Animal Oil*.

Elecampane.—The powdered root of this plant is very popular with grooms and horse doctors, and enters into endless nostrums. It acts as a gentle stimulant, and is very innocent in the quantities in which it is given.

Emetic, Tartar—See *Antimony*.

Epsom Salts.—Not much used in horse medicine.

Ether—Spirit of Nitrous Ether, or Sweet Spirit of Nitre.— This well-known preparation is a valuable one, and extensively used as a diuretic and also as an anti-spasmodic and diaphoretic, so that it is in request for many of the ills the horse suffers from. In colds, influenza, &c., it is given in conjunction with solution of acetate of ammonia, under which a recipe for a fever mixture will be found. When used as an anti-spasmodic in colic 2oz. may be given with 1oz. of laudanum in ale or gruel; and as a diuretic 2oz. may be given at night in the water.

SULPHURIC ETHER is also used in colic or gripes. The dose is ½oz., with a wineglassful of brandy or other spirits, and 1oz. of laudanum; the whole given in at least 1½ pints of water or gruel.

Foxglove.—See *Digitalis*.

Gentian.—This is a bitter tonic and stomachic of great value. The root of the plant (*Gentiana lutea*), dried and ground into a fine powder, is the form in which it is mostly given to the horse, although both the extract and tincture of gentian are also used. Given as a powder with the corn it should be mixed with liquorice powder and some of the carminative and odorous seeds, such as carraway, coriander, or aniseed. And it is often combined with one of the mineral tonics, such as the sulphate of iron or sulphate of copper. The following form for tonic powders will, in cases of debility and loss of appetite, be found useful: *Tonic powders*: Pure sulphate of iron, 1½oz.; powdered gentian root, 3oz.; liquorice powder, 1½oz.; aniseed and carraways ground, each 3oz. The whole well mixed and divided into twelve powders, one of which to be given mixed with the corn—which must be previously slightly damped—each night. The dose of the extract is from ½ to 1 drachm, and of the tincture 1oz. to 2oz., mixed with water.

Ginger.—This article is too well known to require description, it is, however, not so well known that in the form of powder it is largely adulterated, some of the best looking samples being mixed with flour, and the requisite colour given with turmeric. Medicinally it is a stimulant and cordial, and as such is largely used and of great value in horse medicine. It is generally combined with purgatives, as it stimulates the intestines to action, and combined with such tonics as gentian, it is used as a cordial and appetizer, rousing the stomach to energy and provoking the appetite in animals a bit out of health. A couple of teaspoonfuls of good ground ginger is a useful addition to the oatmeal and water or quart of ale which is sometimes given to the hard travelled and flagging horse. It is also useful in combination with ether and ammonia in cases of windy colic, in which cases the tincture of ginger is the best and most convenient form to give it in, the dose being 1oz.

Goulard's Extract.—See *Lead*.

Hartshorn.—See *Ammonia*.

Hellebore.—A powerful drug, entering into most of the formulæ of the old farriers for mange ointment, but its use is not to be recommended. The fresh roots of the black hellebore have been used in fistulous withers and poll evil, but can only be so used without danger by a veterinary surgeon.

Henbane—Very little used, but occasionally substituted for opium, as it does not, like that drug, tend to produce constipation of the bowels. The extract of henbane is the best form to give it in, the dose of which for the horse is one to two drachms.

Hydrochloric Acid.—See *Muriatic Acid*.

Iodide of Iron.—See *Iron*.

Iodide of Mercury.—See *Mercury*.
Iodide of Potassium.—See *Potassium*.
Iodide of Sulphur.—See *Sulphur*.

Iodine.—Chemical compounds of iodine are largely used in veterinary practice. These are principally iodide of iron, iodide of mercury, iodide of potassium, and iodide of sulphur. Iodine itself, simply mixed with spirit of wine, soap liniment, lard, or mild mercurial ointment, is used to excite and disperse glandular swellings, for which an ointment consisting of one part of iodine and eight parts of lard or mild mercurial ointment may be used, the latter being much the most powerful, and such an ointment, but containing only one-third of the above proportion of iodine makes a good hair stimulant when applied with friction to parts denuded of hair.

Iron.—Besides the iodide of iron, to which I shall only briefly refer, there are two other compounds of this metal of considerable importance in veterinary pharmacy, namely,

IODIDE OF IRON is a preparation combining, to some extent, the characteristic properties of both iodine and iron; it is a tonic and a stimulant, increasing the general vigour of the system, but acting so decidedly on the absorbent vessels as to be rather too delicate a substance to be safely administered by other than professional men. The dose of it is half a drachm to a drachm.

SULPHATE OF IRON is the ordinary green copperas, or vitriol of commerce, purified; it exists in crystals of a bright green colour, with a slight bluish tint. It is an astringent and a tonic, and as the latter it is principally used, the dose being from one to two drachms daily; it is usual to give it in conjunction with gentian or some other bitter tonic, and some of the aromatic carmination seeds, such as carraway or coriander. I think the form for tonic powders, given under "gentian," will be found as useful as any compound of the kind. At the Royal College of Veterinary Surgeons the following tonic mass is, I believe, used: *Tonic Mass*: Sulphate of iron, 4oz.; powdered ginger, 2oz.; and common mass (that is, linseed meal and treacle), 10oz.; the dose of which would be from an ounce to an ounce and a half. I think, however, that it is preferable to give it in form of a powder when it can be so readily given with the provender.

TINCTURE OF IRON is also a valuable medicine, and as well as being a tonic, it is a styptic, and so used in hæmorrhages from the kidneys, uterus, and bladder. The dose is half an ounce in half a pint of water.

Laudanum.—See *Opium*.

Lead.—Several compounds of lead are useful in treating horse diseases.

ACETATE OF LEAD, better known by its popular name of *sugar of lead*, is a styptic, and may be given in drachm doses, combined with opium, in cases of internal hæmorrhage; it is also of value in cases of severe and protracted diarrhœa, but it is principally used externally. In ophthalmia and inflammation of the eye, a lotion composed of fifteen to twenty grains in eight ounces of distilled water frequently effects a cure. It is a common mistake to use lotions of sugar of lead much too strong. The country farrier seems generally to act on the belief that if a little of any drug does good, a large quantity will do more.

SOLUTION OF SUBACETATE OF LEAD, commonly called Goulard's Extract, is used in a diluted form; thus, Goulard's Extract two drachms, rectified spirits of wine half an ounce, to distilled water one pint. This is known as Goulard's Lotion; it is used externally for the same purposes as sugar of lead.

Linseed Oil.—A mild laxative dose, a pint and a half; it is a convenient medium for giving turpentine.

Mercury.—There are several preparations of mercury which require mention.

IODIDES OF MERCURY are two compounds of iodine and mercury in use in veterinary practice known as the green iodide, and the red iodide; and it is the latter, which is much the stronger, and that is used in horse practice. The difference must be kept distinctly in mind, as the iodide being used as an application for red mange on the dog, the substitution of the biniodide, as in a case which recently came under my notice, might kill the dog; and if the iodide were used instead of biniodide for the horse, it would be ineffective. The iodide and the ointment made with it is always a dull green or a dirty yellow; the biniodide and its ointment are, more or less, bright red. The red iodide of mercury ointment is used as a blister and counter irritant, but its special value consists in the power it has in facilitating absorption, and thereby reducing abnormal growth, such as splints, curbs, spavins, hardened tumours, &c. It is made by mixing one part of the biniodide with seven parts of lard or spermaceti ointment, and it should be applied with friction daily for a considerable time; but it is necessary to stop its application for a few days when an eruption appears and tenderness of the part has been produced.

BICHLORIDE OF MERCURY, OR CORROSIVE SUBLIMATE, is a still more active, powerful, and dangerous drug than calomel. Indeed, it comes into the category of "deadly poisons;" but of nothing more than of drugs can it be truly said "familiarity breeds contempt." Once whilst enjoying a cup of Barland perry in the kitchen of a west country farm, the servant accidentally knocked something off the mantelshelf, which, falling on the hearthstone, was shivered into thousands of pieces which glistened like atoms of ice. The something was corrosive sublimate, enough to poison every person in the parish, yet it had been allowed to lie about with other odds and ends. This is an instance of a sadly too common practice; I think the use of poisons should be discouraged, and non-poisonous articles substituted for them whenever possible. I do not think there is a single purpose in the stable or the farm to which this very popular, but extremely dangerous, article is put that cannot be as well or better accomplished by non-poisonous, or at least much safer, means. As an application to indolent sores or proud flesh, there are better and safer articles; and for the destruction of parasites on horse and cattle, non-poisonous applications are equally effective.

MERCURIAL OR BLUE OINTMENT is mercury or quicksilver killed by triturition with lard, and is used alone, or with iodine, as an application for the reduction and dispersion of hard swellings, and it is also often used for destroying lice, and enters into many recipes for mange ointments; but I do not recommend it for either of these two latter purposes, as more effectual and less dangerous remedies can be used.

RED PRECIPITATE is a powerful preparation, and one part of it to seven parts of rosin ointment makes an excellent stimulating application to sluggish sores that show an indisposition to heal. For canker in the foot the ointment given under that heading I have found excellent.

WHITE PRECIPITATE, another mercurial, is also used for destroying lice, &c., and an ointment of it is sometimes of good effect applied to indolent sores.

Mindererus's Spirit.—See *Ammonia*.

Monkshood or Wolfsbane (*Aconitum napellus*).—The large blue flowered monkshood is well known as a garden plant. It is native to the Alpine and other mountainous forests. The root and the leaves are both used medicinally, as are, although not so generally, the seeds. From these are made various preparations as the tincture extract and liniment. From them is obtained the active medicinal principle of the plant aconitine. Aconite, whether used internally or externally, acts as a sedative, and is a most useful agent in the hands of the professional man. But it is of too powerfully active and dangerous a nature to be used except under such advice and guidance. The fresh root bears such a resemblance to horse radish that fatal mistakes have occurred through confounding the two.

Mountain Arnica.—See *Arnica*.

Muriate of Ammonia, or Hydrochlorate of Ammonia, commonly called Sal Ammoniac.—See *Ammonia*.

Muriate of Antimony, or Ter-chloride of Antimony, commonly called Butyr of Antimony, and Oil and Butter of Antimony.—See *Antimony*.

Muriatic Acid, or more correctly hydrochloric acid, commonly called spirit of salt, because it is obtained by the action of sulphuric acid on the chloride of sodium (common salt) is occasionally used in veterinary practice as a tonic, largely diluted with water, the dose being one to two drachms, but it is principally as a lithontriptic that the profession have recourse to it. By lithontriptic is meant an agent that will dissolve or break down the stones, which are earthy carbonates that form in the bladder. In such cases it is given in even larger doses, but, of course, always largely diluted. It is used in combination with rectified spirit of wine in making tincture of iron, which preparation is given as an astringent and a styptic. Externally applied, muriatic acid acts as a caustic and antiseptic, and may be usefully applied lightly to foul unhealthy sores.

Mustard Poultice.—To make a mustard poultice : mix with it equal parts or less, according to the stimulation of the part sought to be affected, of linseed meal, and mix them with cold water to the required consistence.

Myrrh is a gum-resin, which—by name at least, is familiar to most people. It is an Eastern product, long known, as is proved by the very frequent reference to it in the Bible. The best myrrh is imported to us from Turkey, and comes in small, irregular roundish pieces, called tears of a reddish-yellow colour, and possessing, to most people, an agreeable, although peculiar odour. It is principally used in form of tincture—that is in solution in spirit and in conjunction with other gums and resins, a good form for which will be found under "Aloes." It is very useful as an application to cuts, for the spirit acts as a styptic, and when it has evaporated it leaves a protective coating of the gum deposited on the surface of the wound. It is also an excellent stimulant to all indolent, unhealthy sores of an ulcerous character, correcting their fœtidness, and inducing healthy granulation.

Nightshade, Deadly.—See *Belladonna*.

Nitrate of Silver.—See *Silver, Nitrate of*.

Nitre.—See *Potash*.

Nitric Acid, often called aqua fortis, although aqua fortis of the shops is a diluted form of nitric acid.—This is a powerful caustic, quickly destroying animal tissue, and is valuable as an application to all fungoid growths and excrescences. It is, therefore, useful in canker of the foot, &c., and is a destroyer of warts where it can be safely applied, but its great fluidity enjoins that it must be skilfully used, otherwise it spreads on to and destroys surrounding healthy tissue. To avoid this it is often used mixed with flowers of sulphur into a paste. A mixture of it with muriatic acid, known as nitro-muriatic acid, is given internally as a tonic and astringent in doses of one drachm largely diluted with water.

Nux Vomica.—The seeds of the poison-nut tree from which strychnine is made. See *Strychnine*.

Oak Bark and Oak Galls, much more used for cattle than horses both are astringents, and owe that quality to the gallic acid or tannic acid which they contain, and these can be used with more precision than the crude bark and galls from which they are obtained.

Oils are animal or vegetable, according to the source from which they are obtained, and they are either fixed or fat oils, or volatile, or essential oils, but the old farriers, like too many modern farmers, use the word as a sort of abracadabra referring to the utterly absurd mixtures they call their "iles" with the pride of ignorance in the possession of a supposed grand secret. Who has not met with the "knowing horsey man" who has a recipe for oils that will cure everything, from a simple cut to a break down. The wonder is not so much that these people deceive themselves, but that in these enlightened days they are still able to impose on intelligent horse owners, who on other points are not only sane but shrewd enough. Most of the nostrums referred to are designated by the colour as black oils, white oils, green oils, red oils, &c.

Oil of Amber is an empyreumatic oil, which often enters into the compounds referred to.

Oil of Bay was another favourite with old practitioners, and, indeed, it once held a place in the Edinburgh Pharmacopœia under the name of *oleum fixum lami nobilis*. It is obtained from the berries of the *Lamus nobilis*, by first saturating them with steam to soften them, and afterwards subjecting them to pressure, when an oil is obtained of about the consietence of melted butter, green in colour, and strongly aromatic both in taste and smell ; it is a stimulant, although a mild one, and as such useful, in combination with more active agents, for sprains and bruises.

Oil of Bricks was the name given to oil that had been first used to saturate a porous brick, and afterwards got from it by subjecting the brick to heat ; of course it was not improved by the process.

Oil of Elder is simply rape or olive oil coloured by boiling or macerating elder leaves in it—or, what is often the case, with cabbage leaves. It is only kept by chemists, on account of its colour, to meet the prejudices of the vulgar.

Oil of Origanum, or Oil of Thyme.—This is an essential oil, distilled from the common marjoram (*Origanum vulgare*), and probably also from the wild thyme, or, as it is called in some localities, mother of thyme (*Thymus sephyllum*). It is much used because of its powerful and, to some people, agreeable odour to disguise mixtures, and to cover the disagreeable smell of other drugs.

Oil of Spikes is the vulgar name for **Oil of Lavender**, an essential or volatile oil, distilled from the flowering spikes of the lavender plant ; it figures frequently in the nostrums of the stable as an ingredient in liniments, but as it is very expensive, rape oil slightly scented with the commonest foreign oil of lavender has to do duty for it.

Oil of Sulphur, or Balsam of Sulphur.—This is made by boiling one part of flower of sulphur in eight parts of olive oil, and is perhaps the most filthy compound ever invented by a quack ; it has been extolled as a specific for coughs of every kind, an expellant of worms, and a certain cure for mange, but it can very well be dispensed with.

Oil of Tar, or Spirit of Tar.—A villainous smelling liquid, worse than tar water ; is a residuum in the distillation of impure pyroligneous acid, and has been vaunted as a cure for mange and other skin affections, but there are cleaner and better remedies.

Oil of Turpentine, or Spirit of Turpentine, is too familiar to need description. It is valuable as an ingredient in stimulating liniments. Internally, it acts as a diuretic when given in repeated doses of 2 drachms to 4 drachms ; and as an anti-spasmodic and a vermifuge it is given in doses of 2oz. to 4oz. It should always be administered in a demulcent, such as linseed oil, with which it readily mixes.

Ointments.—Ointments are combinations of animal fat and fixed oils, with other substances, and forms for making various of them will be found under the names of the substances forming their active character. A useful *Cooling and Healing Ointment* is made by melting together 4oz. olive oil, 4oz. beeswax, and ½lb. fresh hog's lard. In making ointments only sufficient heat to melt the ingredients should be used, and the whole afterwards stirred until cold.

Olive Oil.—This oil is obtained from the ripe fruit of the olive tree, cultivated in Italy, Spain, the south of France, and north of Africa. Under the name of salad oil it is familiar to most people. It is used in making camphorated oil, and enters into the composition of many ointments and liniments. It acts as a laxative on the horse, but very mildly.

Opium.—This is the inspissated juice of the poppy (*Papaver somniferum*) obtained from that plant in Turkey, Egypt, and in India, by making longitudinal incisions in the capsules when nearly ripe, and collecting the juice which exudes, and which is afterwards thickened by exposure to the heat of the sun, and when of the desired consistence made up into irregular lumps, which are covered with the poppy leaves. Opium is one of the most valuable medicines we possess; it is narcotic in its action, and is largely used in all inflammatory diseases, particularly when the bowels, uterus, &c., are the seat of the disease, in which cases it is usually given rubbed down with warm water, the dose for the horse being from 1dr. to 2dr. As an antispasmodic in colic or gripes, &c., the tincture of opium —better known as laudanum—is used, and that generally in combination with either ammonia or turpentine. A convenient form for administering it is given in the recipe for Gripe Tincture (p. 85). The dose of laudanum for the horse is 1oz. to 2oz. It also enters into the composition of many liniments, exercising its influence in allaying local pain and inflammation.

Pimento Berries, sold in the shops as allspice or Jamaica pepper, is a stimulant and tonic—a tincture if it is used in flatulent colic; and the powdered berries are used as an addition to what are called "condition powders," more on account of their aromatic taste and smell than their actual medicinal properties.

Pitch (Burgundy) is a resinous substance got from the spruce fir, which, softened to proper consistence with spirit of turpentine, makes a useful "charge," exercising a stimulating action on indolent sores—a good form for such is Burgundy pitch and Canadian balsam, of each 3 parts spirit of turpentine, 1 part mixed and spread on soft white plaster leather.

Potash, Nitrate of, commonly called nitre or saltpetre. This is the sheet anchor of many horse doctors, by whom it is often abused. Nitrate of potash is a febrifuge and a diuretic; when used as a diuretic it may be given in the water or in a bran mash, ½oz. being a sufficient dose. It is, however, often given in form of ball, for which the following formula will be found to answer: *Diuretic or Staling Balls*

Take powdered nitre 4½oz., finely powdered resin 6oz., powdered ginger 3oz., oil of juniper ½oz., linseed meal and treacle sufficient to make up into twelve convenient sized balls. As a febrifuge it should be given in doses of 1½dr. to 2dr., repeated frequently either in the form of the fever mixture, as given under Solution of Acetate of Ammonia, or in ball form as follows : *Fever Balls* : Take powdered nitrate of potash 1½oz., tartar emetic 3dr., finely powdered camphor 3dr., powdered opium 2dr., carefully mixed, and made into six convenient sized balls with common mass. A saturated solution of nitrate of potash in water is an excellent stimulating application to gangrene wounds.

Potassium, Iodide of, is a most valuable therapeutic agent, acting like all the compounds of iodine on glandular structures, and possessing a marked power in reducing abnormal growths. All these preparations are slow and gradual in their effects, and consequently have to be administered for a length of time, but like many other valuable drugs, it is scarcely safe in the hands of any other than the professional man. It is given in cases of glandular swelling, and also in chronic cough and for roaring and whistling, in doses of twenty to thirty grains dissolved in water. It is popular as a human medicine, and is often taken with a recklessness which ignorance of its real nature and effects can only account for : its value has popularised it, and familiarity has bred contempt; but I must warn readers that it cannot be continuously used with impunity.

Poultices.—These are soft preparations of meal, bran, linseed meal, boiled carrot, &c. The common error in applying poultices is to make them too small and allowing them to get dry and hard ; they should in all cases be of sufficient size to retain the heat a considerable time, and when they lose that and their moisture they should be renewed. Poultices for special objects are made of various materials, as of mustard or mustard and linseed meal mixed, when a stimulation of the parts is aimed at. A poultice of yeast (fresh brewer's barm) is a useful disinfectant to ulcerous sores. A poultice of boiled carrots has a soothing effect on cankerous irritable sores, and various drugs are added to poultices to produce special effects, as : alum or salt as astringents, powdered charcoal or the solutions of the chlorides of lime or soda as disinfectants, and opium, belladonna, &c., as sedatives.

Pyroligneous Acid.—See *Acetic Acid*.

Red Precipitate.—See *Mercury*.

Resin.—Resin is a diuretic, and may be given in doses of from four to six drachms. The practice of giving it in powder mixed with the corn, whether given alone or mixed with other substances under the name of horse powders, &c., is objectionable, as the heat of the mouth softens it and makes it adhere to the teeth, &c. It should, therefore, be given in form of ball, as given under Potash, Nitrate of.

Sal Ammoniac.—See *Ammonia*.

Salt.—See *Sodium*.

Salts, Spirits of.—See *Muriatic Acid*.

Savin Ointment.—This is made by digesting one part of the bruised fresh young tops of savine (*Juniperus sabina*) in two parts of lard, which can be done in a water bath or in a moderately heated oven. If the savin is tied up in a piece of muslin it will render straining of the ointment unnecessary. It is used to keep open blisters and to promote the discharge from setons, for which purpose a little of it is smeared on the tape used.

Silver, Nitrate of—Caustic, or Lunar Caustic.—This, as its name implies, is a caustic, and one of the most valuable and manageable ones. It is used to destroy gangrenous and fungoid growths. In ophthalmia a solution of four or five grains to 1oz. of distilled water is used, a few drops of it being introduced into the eye. In some cases growths on the eye require to be touched with the solid caustic, but this should be done only by a professional man.

Soda, Carbonate of.—This is an antacid, and slightly diuretic; the dose is ½oz.

Sodium, Chloride of, or Common Salt.—With drugs, as with other things, familiarity breeds contempt, and so it comes that owners of horses, cattle, and sheep, neglect this best of tonics and alteratives for some trumped-up quack medicine. When a horse is "off his feed," or weak from the effects of past illness, give him 1oz. of common salt three times a day regularly, sprinkled through his corn.

Spanish Fly.—See *Cantharides*.

Spirit of Nitre, Sweet.—See *Ether*.

Strychnia, or Strychnine.—This is made from nux vomica, or poison nut, and is one of the most powerful medicines we have. It is on that account unsafe in any other than professional hands; although when judiciously administered it is in many cases of the highest value. To the horse it is given in cases of paralysis, acting as a stimulant to the motor nerves. It has the additional advantage, on account of its bitterness—which is of such a persistent character that no one having tasted it can ever forget it—of increasing the appetite and acting as a tonic to the digestive organs. The dose for the horse is from one to three grains, the smaller dose being first tried. It is given combined with such bitter tonics as quassia or gentian, twice a day, and has to be continued some time, its effects on the patients being constantly and carefully watched.

Sugar of Lead.—See *Lead*.

Sulphate of Copper.—See *Copper*.

Sulphate of Zinc.—See *Zinc*.

Sulphur or Brimstone.—The form in which sulphur is used in horse medicine is the sublimed or flowers of sulphur; it enters into most of the popular nostrums for horse powders; it has a mild laxative effect, and is one of the harmless things that stable prejudice honours with its confidence; externally it is useful in skin diseases, in which cases it is used in an infinite variety of combinations; the following is as good as any: *Compound Sulphur Ointment*: Take flowers of sulphur ¾lb., powder of the root of white hellebore 2oz., nitrate of potash ½oz., spirit of tar 4oz., soft soap ½lb., and lard (free from salt) 1½lb., mixed. A common prejudice exists with ignorant persons in favour of *Sulphur vivum*, or black brimstone, but it is really the residuum from the sublimation of the sulphur, is always impure, and sometimes dangerous from the presence of arsenic.

IODIDE OF SULPHUR is used as an internal medicine, but it should only be given under professional advice. In the form of ointment, however, it may be resorted to with perfect safety and good results in cases of ringworm and mange in the horse or any other animal, applying a little of it to the affected part twice a day until a cure is effected. The ointment is made by mixing one part of the iodide of sulphur with seven parts of lard, and it should only be made as required, as it will not keep.

Sulphuric Ether.—See *Ether*.
Sweet Spirit of Nitre.—See *Ether*.
Tar.—This is too well known to need description. The sort referred to here is the northern or Stockholm tar. It is a useful application in thrush, and two parts of it mixed with one part of soft soap and stiffened with linseed meal makes an excellent "stopping for feet," in every way superior to the filthy applications in too general use.

Turpentine.—See *Oil of Turpentine*.
Verdigris.—See *Copper*.
Vitriol, Blue.—See *Copper*.
Vitriol, Green.—See *Iron*.
Vitriol, White.—See *Zinc*.
White Precipitate.—See *Mercury*.
Wolfsbane.—See *Aconite*.
Zinc.—There are few preparations of zinc that need mention. Carbonate of zinc or calamine mixed with six parts of lard makes a cooling ointment, or it may be sprinkled as a powder over ichorous sores.

ACETATE OF ZINC.—To make a solution of this, dissolve 1oz. of sulphate of zinc and 1oz. of superacetate or sugar of lead in 1 gallon of soft water, shake well and pour off the clear liquid, which often proves of great use in reducing swelled legs; for this purpose, the bandage should be thoroughly saturated with the solution and put pretty tightly on and covered with a dry flannel bandage.

CHLORIDE OF ZINC is a powerful disinfectant, destroying the effluvia of putrescence in wounds, and is useful for ordinary disinfecting purposes, but care must be used with it, as it is very poisonous. Sir William Burnet's disinfecting fluid is a solution of chloride of zinc. It is also used as a lotion for open joints and to foul sores. The strength should be 1 grain to 1oz. of distilled water. This is also a good application for canker of the foot, fistulous withers, quittor, &c.

SULPHATE OF ZINC, OR WHITE VITRIOL, exists in small crystals, not unlike Epsom salts; it is used as an eyewash and also as an astringent to various discharges, such as grease.

ODDS AND ENDS,

Containing Provincial and Obsolete Terms, &c.

Anbury.—A term applied to lumps raised by the bite of the gadfly, and other excrescences. The writer of "The Gentleman's Jockey," a book of the seventeenth century, says: "An anbury is a bloody wart on any part of horse's body. Cure is the hot iron. Sear the anbury down to the bottom, then mix a little beaten verdigrease and train oil and anoint the place once a day till it be whole; or take the juice of plantain and mix it with vinegar, honey, and powder of alum, and with it anoint the sore."

Anticor, Anticow.—Described by old writers as a swelling along the breast and belly; extending back to the sheath, says Clater. It is by Bracken and others described as a malignant swelling, which, beginning in the breast, rises in the gullet, threatening suffocation. The name was given because of the swelling first appearing against the heart. It is loosely applied to any affection of the chest. In the "Gentleman's Jockey" it is described as the breast pain, or other sickness proceeding from the heart. These diseases proceed from too rank and gross feeding and much fatness. The signs are, a faltering in his forelegs, an inability to bow down his neck and a trembling all over his body. Cure—Let blood, and give 2 spoonfu's diapente in a quart of ale or beer two mornings together.

Bishoping.—This is the cant term applied to the practice of horse copers who alter the apparent age of the horse by tampering with his teeth.

Bitch-Daughter.—When a horse was ill from gross feeding, or overdone by hard work and hard usage, superstition said it was ridden by the "Bitch-daughter," an evil spirit, a meaningless but comfortable way of overlooking their own neglect; and to cure it a sickle, a horseshoe, and a hollow stone were hung over his back. This practice is referred to in Butler's "Hudibras," when speaking of the quack doctor "Sidrophel":

> Chase evil spirits away by dint
> Of sickle, horseshoe, hollow flint.

Dr. Bracken, in his "Art of Farriery Improved," sagely remarks, "If the master will not feed hard when he rides hard, the horse he rides may be truly said to be rid by the 'Bitch-daughter,' or a worse fiend."

Bleeding Horses.—Bleeding was formerly resorted to for every ailment, and that not only as a cure, but as a preventive of disease. We might almost say phlebotomy was a species of worship of our forefathers, and it had its regular feast days, when the life blood of the poor animals was poured out to honour and propitiate a god of their own ignorant creation. Greatest of these feast days was St. Stephen's Day. The following quaint lines from Tusser's "Five Hundred Points of Husbandry" are illustrative of the practice:

> Yer, Christmas be past, let horsse be let blood,
> For mannie a purpose it doocth him much good;
> The day of St. Steeven old fathers did use,
> If that do mislike thee, some other day choose.

The practice is said to have been brought into this country by the Danes. On St. Stephen's Day the Pope's stud was physicked and bled, St. Stephen being the patron saint of horses.

The following lines, from "Neogeorgus's Popish Kingdom," throw some light on the subject, but the writer evidently had no faith:

> Then followeth St. Stephen's Day, whereon doth every man
> His horses jaunt and course abroad as swiftly as he can,
> Until they do extremely sweat, and then they let them blood;
> For this being done upon this day, they say doth do them good,
> And keepes them from all maladies and sicknesse through the yeare,
> As if that Steven any time took charge of horses heare.

Captain.—A captain is a broken-winded or other unsound winded horse, got up for sale to be palmed on the unwary.

Chest-founder.—A term wrongly applied to founder in the feet. The local inflammation of founder in the feet often becomes general, hence, probably, the common error.

Colt Evil.—A discharge from the penis, accompanied by swelling of the sheath and testicles, often caused by allowing young ungelded colts to run loose with mares.

Cord and Crick of the Neck.—Stiffness of the neck muscles from cold the former term applies to a stage of strangles.

Cropping.—The barbarous practice of cropping the ears of horses at one time obtained in this country; nothing can be said too strong in condemnation of leaving the internal ear of an animal exposed; our horsemen have given it up, but with many breeds of dogs the taste (?) of the owners still decrees that the external ear, which nature has provided as a protection to a most delicate organ, shall be cut away in obedience to a vulgar fancy.

Crown Scabs.—Applied to a scurfiness and humourous discharge round the coronet. It should be treated in the same way as Grease.

Docking is the shortening of the substance of the tail.

Falling Evil, or Falling Sickness (also called Planet-struck, Nightmare, or Palsy).

Feltoric.—Another name for Anticor or Anticow.

Frettige.—Another name for founder.

Grogginess.—A term applied to a horse when he goes unsteady and blunderingly without apparent cause. It is also called surbaiting, and may be caused by hard travel on macadamised roads, battering the hoofs, and producing stiffness and inflammation of the legs. It is characterised by a tottering gait or knuckling of the fetlock joint, showing weakness, and is often associated with disease of the navicular bone, or the tendon running over it.

Grunters are horses unsound in wind.

Hammer and Pincers.—A term applied to horses overreaching and striking the fore heels with the hind toes.

Hungry Evil.—Over greediness in eating is so called, but, of course, it is only a symptom, not a disease.

Interfering or Shackle Galls.—Striking one leg against the other. Shackle galling is any galling under the fetlock.

Javart.—Another name for quittor.

Kernels in the Throat.—Lumps, as strangles.

Lask, or Bloody Flux.—Dysentery.

Matlong.—An ulcer on the coronet.

Moon-eye.—Dimness of sight, often preceding a cataract.

Mules.—Rats'-tails, which see.

Nicking.—Four or five cuts, one made across the under side of the tail—the object was to produce a cock-tail.

Oslets.—A kind of splint near the knee bone on the inside is so called.

Pearl Pin and Web.—A film on the eye, dimming the sight.

Quidding.—Chewing the food into balls, and dropping it out of the mouth.

Rats' Tails.—Excrescences discharging ichorous matter, extending from the middle of the shank to the fetlock.

Scrupin.—A splint.

Sleeping Evil.—Stomach staggers.

Tetters.—A cutaneous disease, with itchiness, prurigo.

Vives.—A swelling of the glands under the ears, often ending in a tumour.

Wolves' Teeth.—Sometimes called eye teeth, a small tooth appearing on upper jaw about an inch from the grinders, which should be removed. The term is also applied to teeth that grow in such a manner as to prick and wound the tongue or gums—this arises from the teeth meeting, the upper often overlapping the under, and consequently not being ground level—these *wolves' teeth* are mostly seen in old horses, and their points should be filed.

ELLIMAN'S ROYAL EMBROCATION.

For Sprains, Curbs, and Splints, when forming.
For Overreaches, Chapped Heels, Wind Galls.
For Rheumatism in Horses.
For Broken Knees, Bruises, Capped Hocks.

For Sore Throats and Influenza.
For Sore Shoulders, Sore Backs.
For Sore Mouths in Sheep and Lambs.
For Sprains, Cuts, and Bruises in Dogs.

REMARKS BY MASTERS OF HOUNDS.

I think it very useful.
      RUTLAND.
      Master of Belvoir Hounds.

Indispensable in any stable, but especially in the stable of a Master of Hounds.
      HADDINGTON,
      Master of Berwickshire Hounds.

I find this a very useful application for cuts, strains, and bruises in horses' legs.
      C. PRYSE (Colonel),
      Master of Colonel Pryse's Hounds.

Gives much satisfaction.
      FRANCIS F. LOVELL,
      Master of New Forest Stag Hounds.

Exceedingly good for sprains and cuts in horses, and also for cuts in hounds' feet.—Yours faithfully,
      J. M. BROWNE (Major),
      Master of South Staffordshire Hounds.

I consider it a good thing for strains and bruises.
      E. R. SWORDER,
      Master of East Kent Hounds.

Sold by Chemists and Saddlers, Price 2s., 2s. 6d., 3s. 6d.
PREPARED ONLY BY
ELLIMAN, SONS, & CO. Slough, England.

Health and Vigour for Dogs

GUARANTEED BY THE USE OF

CLARKE'S
BUFFALO MEAT BISCUITS

As used in ROYAL KENNELS and most of the Leading Kennels throughout the World.

Gold Medal, Vienna; Highest Award, Calcutta; Prize Medal, International Exhibition, London, 1884; Fifteen Gold, Silver, and Bronze Medals.

FRANK GOODALL, the Queen's Huntsman, writes: "Your BUFFALO BISCUITS have convinced me that a more nourishing and suitable Food for Dogs has not yet been invented, combining, as they do, all the qualities of a most perfect food; and to all that desire to keep their Dogs in good health and condition I can with the greatest confidence recommend them.—Yours truly, FRANK GOODALL."

BUFFALO GREYHOUND BISCUITS.—These contain 30 to 40 per cent. of Meat, and are particularly adapted for Greyhounds in Training.

CLARKE'S BUFFALO PUPPY CAKES.—The Buffalo Puppy Cakes are Manufactured with Milk, and are recommended for all Young Dogs.

CLARKE'S BUFFALO TOY DOG CAKES.—These Cakes are Manufactured with Milk, the fine particles of Meat and Gravy possess great nourishment, and are easily masticated and digested.

ROUND OATMEAL DOG BISCUITS.—Recommended where Flesh is used for Dogs in Training.

PLAIN ROUND DOG BISCUITS.—Intended for use where Flesh is used in preference to Meat Biscuits, or alone as a Summer Diet, and for Dogs out of Training.

CLARKE'S PUPPY FOOD.—For Puppies immediately after birth. In 1lb. Packets.

CLARKE'S PERFECTION DOG SOAP is unequalled for Cleansing and Purifying the Skin. Sold in Boxes of Three Tablets, 1s. per box.

DOG COLLARS, CHAINS, LEADS, MUZZLES, WHIPS, &c. KENNELS, TRAVELLING BOXES, FEEDING TROUGHS, AND OTHER APPLIANCES.

ANCHOR PATENT BISCUIT WORKS,
Limehouse, London, E.

Catalogue of Practical Handbooks Published by L. Upcott Gill, 170, Strand, London, W.C.

ANGLER, BOOK OF THE ALL-ROUND. A Comprehensive Treatise on Angling in both Fresh and Salt Water. In Four Divisions, as named below. By JOHN BICKERDYKE. With over 220 Engravings. *In cloth, price* 5s. 6d. (A few copies of a LARGE PAPER EDITION, *bound in Roxburghe, price* 25s.; *the price will shortly be raised to* 30s.).

Angling for Coarse Fish. A very Complete and Practical Work on Bottom Fishing, according to the Methods in use on the Thames, Trent, Norfolk Broads, and elsewhere. Illustrated. *Price* 1s., *cloth* 2s. (*uncut*).

Angling for Pike. A Practical and Comprehensive Work on the most Approved Methods of Fishing for Pike or Jack; including an Account of Some New Tackles for Spinning, Live-baiting, and Trolling. Profusely Illustrated. *Price* 1s., *cloth* 2s. (*uncut*).

Angling for Game Fish. A Practical Treatise on the Various Methods of Fishing for Salmon; Moorland, Chalk-stream, and Thames Trout; Grayling, and Char. Well Illustrated. *Price* 1s. 6d., *cloth* 2s. 6d. (*uncut*).

Angling in Salt Water. A Practical Work on Sea Fishing with Rod and Line, from the Shore, Piers, Jetties, Rocks, and from Boats; together with Some Account of Hand-Lining. Over 50 Engravings. *Price* 1s., *cloth* 2s. (*uncut*).

AQUARIA, MARINE: Their Construction, Arrangement, and Management. Fully Illustrated. By R. A. R. BENNETT, B.A. *In cloth gilt, price* 2s. 6d.

BEE-KEEPING, BOOK OF. A very Practical and Complete Manual on the Proper Management of Bees, especially written for Beginners and Amateurs who have but a few Hives. Fully Illustrated. By W. B. WEBSTER, First-class Expert, B.B.K.A. *Price* 1s.; *cloth,* 1s. 6d.

BEES AND BEE-KEEPING: Scientific and Practical. By F. R. CHESHIRE, F.L.S., F.R.M.S., Lecturer on Apiculture at South Kensington. *In two vols., price* 16s.

Vol. I., Scientific. A complete Treatise on the Anatomy and Physiology of the Hive Bee. *In cloth gilt, price* 7s. 6d.

Vol. II., Practical Management of Bees. An Exhaustive Treatise on Advanced Bee-Culture. *In cloth gilt, price* 8s. 6d.

BICYCLES AND TRICYCLES OF THE YEAR. Descriptions of the New Inventions and Improvements for the Present Season. Designed to assist intending purchasers in the choice of a machine. Illustrated. By HARRY HEWITT GRIFFIN. Twelfth Annual Issue, for 1889. *In paper, price* 1s.

*** All Books Post Free.

BOAT BUILDING AND SAILING, PRACTICAL. Containing Full Instructions for Designing and Building Punts, Skiffs, Canoes, Sailing Boats, &c. Particulars of the most Suitable Sailing Boats and Yachts for Amateurs, and Instructions for their Proper Handling. Fully Illustrated with Designs and Working Diagrams. By ADRIAN NEISON, C.E., DIXON KEMP, A.I.N.A., and G. CHRISTOPHER DAVIES. *In one vol., cloth gilt, price* 7s. 6d.

BOAT BUILDING FOR AMATEURS, PRACTICAL. Containing Full Instructions for Designing and Building Punts, Skiffs, Canoes, Sailing Boats, &c. Fully Illustrated with Working Diagrams. By ADRIAN NEISON, C.E. Second Edition, Revised and Enlarged by DIXON KEMP, Author of "Yacht Designing," "A Manual of Yacht and Boat Sailing," &c. *In cloth gilt, price* 2s. 6d.

BOAT SAILING FOR AMATEURS. Containing Particulars of the most Suitable Sailing Boats and Yachts for Amateurs, and Instructions for their Proper Handling, &c. Illustrated with numerous Diagrams. By G. CHRISTOPHER DAVIES. Second Edition, Revised and Enlarged, and with several New Plans of Yachts. *In cloth gilt, price* 5s.

BOOKBINDING FOR AMATEURS: Being Descriptions of the various Tools and Appliances Required, and Minute Instructions for their Effective Use. By W. J. E. CRANE. Illustrated with 156 Engravings. *In cloth gilt, price* 2s. 6d.

BROADS, THE LAND OF THE. By E. R. SUFFLING.
  ILLUSTRATED EDITION.—The most Complete Guide to the whole of the District—embracing the Broads and their Waterways of Norfolk and Suffolk—that has yet been published. With a good Map, *printed in four* colours. *Price* 2s. 6d.
  CHEAP EDITION.—An abridged Edition, with Plates of Characteristic Sketches by J. TEMPLE. A good and *clear* Map, in black and white, is also given. *In Coloured Cover, price* 1s.

BUTTERFLIES AND MOTHS, COLLECTING: Being Directions for Capturing, Killing, and Preserving Lepidoptera and their Larvæ. Illustrated. Reprinted, with Additions, from "Practical Taxidermy." By MONTAGU BROWNE. *In paper, price* 1s.

CACTUS CULTURE FOR AMATEURS: Being Descriptions of the various Cactuses grown in this country; with Full and Practical Instructions for their Successful Cultivation. By W. WATSON, Assistant Curator of the Royal Botanic Gardens, Kew. Profusely Illustrated. *In cloth gilt, price* 5s.

CAGE BIRDS, BRITISH. Containing Full Directions for Successfully Breeding, Rearing, and Managing the various British Birds that can be kept in Confinement. Illustrated with COLOURED PLATES and numerous finely-cut Wood Engravings. By R. L. WALLACE. *In cloth gilt, price* 10s. 6d.

CAGE BIRDS, DISEASES OF: Their Causes, Symptoms, and Treatment. A Handbook for everyone who keeps a Bird. By DR. W. T. GREENE, F.Z.S. *In paper, price* 1s.

*** All Books Post Free.**

CANARY BOOK. Containing Full Directions for the Breeding, Rearing, and Management of all Varieties of Canaries and Canary Mules, the Promotion and Management of Canary Societies and Exhibitions, and all other matters connected with this Fancy. By ROBERT L. WALLACE. Second Edition, Enlarged and Revised, with many new Illustrations of Prize Birds, Cages, &c. *In cloth gilt, price* 5s.*;* with *Coloured Plates,* 6s. 6d.*;* and in Sections as follows :

 Canaries, General Management of. Including Cages and Cage-making, Breeding, Managing, Mule Breeding, Diseases and their Treatment, Moulting, Rats and Mice, &c. Illustrated. *In cloth, price* 2s. 6d.

 Canaries, Exhibition. Containing Full Particulars of all the different Varieties, their Points of Excellence, Preparing Birds for Exhibition, Formation and Management of Canary Societies and Exhibitions. Illustrated. *In cloth, price* 2s. 6d.

CARD TRICKS, BOOK OF, for Drawing-room and Stage Entertainments by Amateurs ; with an Exposure of Tricks as practised by Card Sharpers and Swindlers. Numerous Illustrations. By Prof. R. KUNARD. *Illustrated Wrapper, price* 2s. 6d.

CHURCH EMBROIDERY: Its Early History and Manner of Working ; Materials Used and Stitches Employed ; Raised and Flat Couching, Appliqué, &c., &c., including Church Work over Cardboard. A practical handbook for Church Workers. Illustrated. *In paper, price* 1s.

CHURCH FESTIVAL DECORATIONS. Comprising Directions and Designs for the Suitable Decoration of Churches for Christmas, Easter, Whitsuntide, and Harvest. Illustrated. A useful book for the Clergy and their Lay Assistants. *In paper, price* 1s.

COINS, A GUIDE TO ENGLISH PATTERN, in Gold, Silver, Copper, and Pewter, from Edward I. to Victoria, with their Value. By the REV. G. F. CROWTHER, M.A. Illustrated. *In silver cloth, with gilt facsimiles of Coins, price* 5s.

COINS OF GREAT BRITAIN AND IRELAND, A GUIDE TO THE, in Gold, Silver, and Copper, from the Earliest Period to the Present Time, with their Value. By the late Colonel W. STEWART THORBURN. Of immense value to collectors and dealers. 27 Plates in Gold, Silver, and Copper, and 8 Plates of Gold and Silver Coins in RAISED FACSIMILE. *In cloth, with silver facsimiles of Coins, price* 7s. 6d.

COLLIE, THE. Its History, Points, and Breeding. By HUGH DALZIEL. Illustrated. *Demy 8vo, price* 1s.*; cloth,* 2s.

CONJURING, BOOK OF MODERN. A Practical Guide to Drawing-room and Stage Magic for Amateurs. By PROFESSOR R. KUNARD. Illustrated. *Price* 2s. 6d.

COOKERY FOR AMATEURS ; or, French Dishes for English Homes of all Classes. Includes Simple Cookery, Middle-class Cookery, Superior Cookery, Cookery for Invalids, and Breakfast and Luncheon Cookery. By MADAME VALÉRIE. Second Edition. *In paper, price* 1s.

※ **All Books Post Free.**

CUCUMBER CULTURE FOR AMATEURS. Including also Melons, Vegetable Marrows, and Gourds. Illustrated. By W. J. MAY. *In paper, price 1s.*

DEGREES, A GUIDE TO, in Arts, Science, Literature, Law, Music, and Divinity, in the United Kingdom, the Colonies, the Continent, and the United States. By E. WOOTON, Author of "A Guide to the Medical Profession," &c. *In cloth, price 15s.*

DOGS, BREAKING AND TRAINING: Being Concise Directions for the proper Education of Dogs, both for the Field and for Companions. Second Edition. By "PATHFINDER." With Chapters by HUGH DALZIEL on Work of Special Breeds; Trail or Drag Hounds; Training Bloodhounds; Defenders and Watch Dogs; Sheep Dogs—Stock Tenders; Life Savers—Water Dogs; Vermin Destroyers; House Manners; Behaviour Out of Doors. Illustrated. *In cloth gilt, price 6s. 6d.*

DOGS, BRITISH: Their Varieties, History, and Characteristics By HUGH DALZIEL, assisted by Eminent Fanciers. NEW EDITION, Revised and Enlarged. Illustrated with First-class COLOURED PLATES and full-page Engravings of Dogs of the Day. This is the fullest and most recent work on the various breeds of dogs kept in England. In two Volumes, *Demy 8vo, price 10s. 6d.* each, as follows:

Dogs Used in Field Sports. Containing Particulars of the following, among other Breeds: Greyhound, Irish Wolfhound, Bloodhound, Foxhound, Harrier, Basset, Dachshund, Pointer, Setters, Spaniels, and Retrievers. SEVEN COLOURED PLATES and 21 full-page Engravings. *In cloth gilt, price 10s. 6d.*

Dogs Useful to Man in other Work than Field Sports; House and Toy Dogs. Containing Particulars of the following, among other Breeds: Collie, Bulldog, Mastiff, St. Bernard, Newfoundland, Great Dane, Fox and all other Terriers, King Charles and Blenheim Spaniels, Pug, Pomeranian, Poodle, Italian Greyhound, Toy Dogs, &c., &c. COLOURED PLATES and full-page Engravings. *In cloth gilt, price 10s. 6d.*

DOGS, DISEASES OF: Their Causes, Symptoms, and Treatment; Modes of Administering Medicines; Treatment in cases of Poisoning, &c. For the use of Amateurs. By HUGH DALZIEL. Second Edition. *In paper, price 1s.; in cloth gilt, 2s.*

DUCKS AND GEESE: Their Characteristics, Points, and Management. Splendidly Illustrated. *In paper, price 1s. 6d.*

EXHIBITION ACCOUNT BOOKS. For use at all Dog, Poultry, Rabbit, and Cage Bird Shows. In Four Books, comprising: I. Minute Book; II. Cash Book; III. Entries Book; IV. Ledger. With Full Directions, and Illustrative Examples for Working them. N.B.—The Set of Four Books is kept in Three Series: No. 1, for Show of 500 Entries, 5s. the Set; No. 2, for 1000 Entries, 7s. 6d. the Set; and No. 3, for 1500 Entries, 12s. 6d. the Set. Larger sizes in proportion. The books can be had separate. MINUTE

✱ **All Books Post Free.**

BOOK—No. 1, 1s.; No. 2, 1s. 3d.; No. 3, 2s. CASH BOOK—No. 1, 2s.; No. 2, 2s. 6d.; No. 3, 4s. ENTRIES BOOK—No. 1, 2s.; No. 2, 2s. 6d.; No. 3, 4s. Ledger—No. 1, 2s.; No. 2, 2s. 6d.; No. 3, 4s.

FANCY WORK SERIES, ARTISTIC. A Series of Illustrated Manuals on Artistic and Popular Fancy Work of various kinds. Each number is complete in itself, and issued at the uniform *price* of 6d. Now ready—(1) MACRAMÉ LACE (Second Edition); (2) PATCHWORK; (3) TATTING; (4) CREWEL WORK; (5) APPLIQUÉ; (6) FANCY NETTING.

FERNS, CHOICE BRITISH. Descriptive of the most beautiful Variations from the common forms, and their Culture. By C. T. DRUERY, F.L.S. Very accurate PLATES, and other Illustrations. *In cloth gilt, price 2s. 6d.*

FERRETS AND FERRETING. Containing Instructions for the Breeding, Management, and Working of Ferrets. Second Edition, Re-written and greatly Enlarged. Illustrated. *In paper, price 6d.*

FERTILITY OF EGGS CERTIFICATE. These are Forms of Guarantee given by the Sellers to the Buyers of Eggs for Hatching. undertaking to refund value of any unfertile eggs, or to replace them with good ones. Very valuable to sellers of eggs, as they induce purchases. *In books, with counterfoils, price 6d.*

FIREWORK-MAKING FOR AMATEURS. A most complete, accurate, and easily-understood work on Making both Simple and High-class Fireworks. By Dr. W. H. BROWNE, M.A. *Price 2s. 6d.*

FOX TERRIER STUD BOOK. Vol. I., containing the Pedigree of every Fox Terrier that Won a Prize at any of the Principal Shows in 1888. Over 1400 Entries of Leading Dogs. Edited by HUGH DALZIEL. *In cloth, price 2s. 6d.*

FOX TERRIER, THE. Its History, Points, Breeding, Rearing, Preparing for Exhibition, and Coursing. By HUGH DALZIEL. Illustrated. *Price 1s.; cloth, 2s.*

GAME AND GAME SHOOTING, NOTES ON. Miscellaneous Observations on Birds and Animals, and on the Sport they afford for the Gun in Great Britain, including Grouse, Partridges, Pheasants, Hares, Rabbits, Quails, Woodcocks, Snipe, and Rooks. By J. J. MANLEY, M.A. Illustrated. *In cloth gilt, 400pp., price 7s. 6d.*

GAME PRESERVING, PRACTICAL. Containing the fullest Directions for Rearing and Preserving both Winged and Ground Game, and Destroying Vermin; with other Information of Value to the Game Preserver. Illustrated. By WILLIAM CARNEGIE. *In cloth gilt, demy 8vo, price 21s.*

GARDENING, DICTIONARY OF. A Practical Encyclopædia of Horticulture, for Amateurs and Professionals. Illustrated with upwards of 2440 Engravings. Edited by G. NICHOLSON, Curator of the Royal Botanic Gardens, Kew; assisted by Prof. Trail, M.D., Rev. P. W. Myles, B.A., F.L.S., W. Watson, J. Garrett, and other Specialists. *In 4 vols., large post 4to.*

* **All Books Post Free.**

Vol. I., A to E, 552pp., 743 Illustrations; Vol. II., F to O, 544pp., 811 Illustrations; Vol. III., P to S, 537pp., 564 Illustrations; Vol. IV., T to Z, and Supplement of Pronouncing Dictionary, Indices to Plants for Special Purposes, Recent Introductions, &c. 322 Illustrations. *Price* 15s. *each. In Monthly Parts, price* 2s. 6d.

GARDEN PESTS AND THEIR ERADICATION. Containing Practical Instructions for the Amateur to overcome the Enemies of the Garden. Illustrated. *In paper, price* 1s.

GOAT, BOOK OF THE. Containing Full Particulars of the various Breeds of Goats, and their Profitable Management. With many Plates. By H. STEPHEN HOLMES PEGLER. Third Edition, with Engravings and Coloured Frontispiece. *Cloth gilt, price* 4s. 6d.

GOAT-KEEPING FOR AMATEURS: Being the Practical Management of Goats for Milking Purposes. Abridged from "The Book of the Goat," by H. S. HOLMES PEGLER. Illustrated. *In paper, price* 1s.

GREENHOUSE MANAGEMENT FOR AMATEURS. Descriptions of the best Greenhouses and Frames, with Instructions for Building them, particulars of the various methods of Heating, Illustrated Descriptions of the most suitable Plants, with general and special Cultural Directions, and all necessary information for the Guidance of the Amateur. Second Edition, Revised and Enlarged. Magnificently Illustrated. By W. J. MAY. *In cloth gilt, price* 5s.

GREYHOUND, THE: Its History, Points, Breeding, Rearing, Training, and Running. By HUGH DALZIEL. With Coloured Frontispiece. *In cloth gilt, demy* 8vo, *price* 2s. 6d.

GUINEA PIG, THE, for Food, Fur, and Fancy. Illustrated with Coloured Frontispiece and Engravings. An exhaustive book on the Varieties of the Guinea Pig, and its Management. By C. CUMBERLAND, F.Z.S. *In cloth gilt, price* 2s. 6d.

HANDWRITING, CHARACTER INDICATED BY. With Illustrations in Support of the Theories advanced taken from Autograph Letters of Statesmen, Lawyers, Soldiers, Ecclesiastics, Authors, Poets, Musicians, Actors, and other persons. Second Edition. By R. BAUGHAN. *In cloth gilt, price* 2s. 6d.

HARDY PERENNIALS and Old-fashioned Garden Flowers. Descriptions, alphabetically arranged, of the most desirable Plants for Borders, Rockeries, and Shrubberies, including Foliage as well as Flowering Plants. Profusely Illustrated. By J. WOOD. *In cloth, price* 5s.

HOME MEDICINE AND SURGERY: A Dictionary of Diseases and Accidents, and their proper Home Treatment. For Family Use. By W. J. MACKENZIE, M.D., C.M., &c. Illustrated. *In cloth, price* 2s. 6d.

HORSE-KEEPING FOR AMATEURS. A Practical Manual on the Management of Horses, for the guidance of those who keep them for their personal use. By FOX RUSSELL. *Price* 1s.; *cloth,* 2s.

☞ **All Books Post Free.**

HORSES, DISEASES OF: Their Causes, Symptoms, and Treatment. For the use of Amateurs. By HUGH DALZIEL. *In paper, price* 1s.; *cloth,* 2s.

JOURNALISM, PRACTICAL: How to Enter Thereon and Succeed. A Manual for Beginners and Amateurs. A book for all who think of "writing for the Press." By JOHN DAWSON. *In cloth gilt, price* 2s. 6d.

LEGAL PROFESSION, A GUIDE TO THE. A Practical Treatise on the various Methods of Entering either Branch of the Legal Profession; also a Course of Study for each of the Examinations, and selected Papers of Questions; forming a Complete Guide to every Department of Legal Preparation. By J. H. SLATER, Barrister-at-Law, of the Middle Temple. *Price* 7s. 6d.

LIBRARY MANUAL, THE. A Guide to the Formation of a Library and the Valuation of Rare and Standard Books. By J. H. SLATER, Barrister-at-Law. Second Edition. *In cloth, price* 2s. 6d.

LILY OF THE VALLEY: All About It, and How to Grow It; Forced Indoors and Out of Doors, in Various Ways. By WILLIAM ROBERTS. *In paper covers, price* 6d.

MICE, FANCY: Their Varieties, Management, and Breeding. Re-issue, with Criticisms and Notes by DR. CARTER BLAKE. Illustrated. *In paper, price* 6d.

MODEL YACHTS AND BOATS: Their Designing, Making, and Sailing. Illustrated with 118 Designs and Working Diagrams. A splendid book for boys and others interested in making and rigging toy boats for sailing. It is the best book on the subject now published. By J. DU V. GROSVENOR. *In leatherette, price* 5s.

MONKEYS, NOTES ON PET, and How to Manage Them. Profusely Illustrated. By ARTHUR PATTERSON. *Cloth gilt, price* 2s. 6d.

MUSHROOM CULTURE FOR AMATEURS. With Full Directions for Successful Growth in Houses, Sheds, Cellars, and Pots, on Shelves, and Out of Doors. Illustrated. By W. J. MAY. *In paper, price* 1s.

NATURAL HISTORY SKETCHES among the Carnivora — Wild and Domesticated; with Observations on their Habits and Mental Faculties. By ARTHUR NICOLS, F.G.S., F.R.G.S. Illustrated. *In cloth gilt, price* 5s.

NEEDLEWORK, DICTIONARY OF. An Encyclopædia of Artistic, Plain, and Fancy Needlework; Plain, practical, complete, and magnificently Illustrated. By S. F. A. CAULFEILD and B. C. SAWARD. Accepted by H.M. the Queen, H.R.H. the Princess of Wales, H.R.H. the Duchess of Edinburgh, H.R.H. the Duchess of Connaught, and H.R.H. the Duchess of Albany Dedicated by special permission to H.R.H. Princess Louise, Marchioness of Lorne. *In demy 4to, 528pp., 829 Illustrations, extra cloth gilt, plain edges, cushioned bevelled boards, price* 21s.; *with COLOURED PLATES, elegant satin brocade cloth binding, and coloured edges* 31s. 6d.

※ **All Books Post Free.**

ORCHIDS: THEIR CULTURE AND MANAGEMENT, with Descriptions of all the Kinds in General Cultivation. Illustrated by Coloured Plates and Engravings. By W. WATSON, Assistant-Curator, Royal Botanic Gardens, Kew. *In Monthly Parts, price* 1s.

PAINTING, DECORATIVE. A Practical Handbook on Painting and Etching upon Textiles, Pottery, Porcelain, Paper, Vellum, Leather, Glass, Wood, Stone, Metals, and Plaster, for the Decoration of our Homes. By B. C. SAWARD. *Cheap Edition, price* 5s.

PARROTS, THE SPEAKING. The Art of Keeping and Breeding the principal Talking Parrots in Confinement. By Dr. KARL RUSS. Illustrated with COLOURED PLATES and Engravings. *In cloth gilt, price* 5s.

PATIENCE, GAMES OF, for one or more Players. A very clearly-written and well-illustrated Book of Instructions on How to Play no less than FORTY different Games of Patience. By Miss WHITMORE JONES. Illustrated. Second Edition. *Price* 1s.

PHEASANT-KEEPING FOR AMATEURS. A Practical Handbook on the Breeding, Rearing, and General Management of Fancy Pheasants in Confinement. By GEO. HORNE. Illustrated with Diagrams of the necessary Pens, Aviaries, &c., and a COLOURED FRONTISPIECE and many full-page Engravings of the chief Varieties of Pheasants, drawn from life by A. F. LYDON. *In cloth gilt, price* 3s. 6d.

PIANOFORTES, TUNING AND REPAIRING. The Amateur's Guide to the Practical Management of a Piano without the intervention of a Professional. By CHARLES BABBINGTON. *In paper, price* 6d.

PICTURE-FRAME MAKING FOR AMATEURS. Being Practical Instructions in the Making of various kinds of Frames for Paintings, Drawings, Photographs, and Engravings. Illustrated. By the REV. J. LUKIN. Cheap Edition, *in paper, price* 1s.

PIG, BOOK OF THE. Containing the Selection, Breeding, Feeding, and Management of the Pig; the Treatment of its Diseases; the Curing and Preserving of Hams, Bacon, and other Pork Foods; and other information appertaining to Pork Farming. By Professor JAMES LONG. Fully Illustrated with Portraits of Prize Pigs by HARRISON WEIR and other Artists, Plans of Model Piggeries, &c. *In cloth gilt, price* 10s. 6d.

PIGEONS, FANCY. Containing Full Directions for the Breeding and Management of Fancy Pigeons, and Descriptions of every known Variety, together with all other information of interest or use to Pigeon Fanciers. Third Edition, bringing the subject down to the present time. 18 COLOURED PLATES, and 22 other full-page Illustrations. By J. C. LYELL. *In cloth gilt, price* 10s. 6d.

*** All Books Post Free.**

POKER BOOK, THE. A Practical Book on Playing the Fascinating American Game of Poker with Success. By R. GUERNDALE. *Price* 1s.

POOL, GAMES OF. Describing Various English and American Pool Games, and giving the Rules in full. Illustrated. *Price* 1s.

POULTRY AND PIGEON DISEASES: Their Causes. Symptoms, and Treatment. A Practical Manual for all Fanciers. *Price* 1s.

POULTRY FOR PRIZES AND PROFIT. Contains: Breeding Poultry for Prizes, Exhibition Poultry, and Management of the Poultry Yard. Handsomely Illustrated. New Edition, Revised and Enlarged. By Professor JAMES LONG. *Cheap Edition, in cloth gilt, price* 2s. 6d.

RABBIT, BOOK OF THE. A Complete Work on Breeding and Rearing all Varieties of Fancy Rabbits, giving their History Variations, Uses, Points, Selection, Mating, Management, &c., &c. NEW EDITION, Revised and Enlarged. Edited by KEMPSTER W. KNIGHT. With an additional chapter on "Hutch Rabbit Farming in the Open," by MAJOR MORANT. Illustrated with Coloured and other Plates. *One handsome vol., price* 10s. 6d.

RABBITS, DISEASES OF: Their Causes, Symptoms, and Cure. With a Chapter on THE DISEASES OF CAVIES. Reprinted from "The Book of the Rabbit" and "The Guinea Pig for Food, Fur, and Fancy." *In paper, price* 1s.

RABBIT-FARMING, PROFITABLE. A Practical Manual, showing how Hutch Rabbit-farming in the Open can be made to Pay Well. By Major G. F. MORANT. Reprinted from "The Book of the Rabbit." *In paper, price* 1s.

RABBITS FOR PRIZES AND PROFIT. Containing Full Directions for the Proper Management of Fancy Rabbits in Health and Disease, for Pets or the Market, and Descriptions of every known Variety, with Instructions for Breeding Good Specimens Illustrated. By CHARLES RAYSON. *In cloth gilt, price* 2s. 6d. Also in Sections, as follows:—

Rabbits, General Management of. Including Hutches Breeding, Feeding, Diseases and their Treatment, Rabbit Coverts, &c. Fully Illustrated. *In paper, price* 1s.

Rabbits, Exhibition. Being descriptions of all Varieties of Fancy Rabbits, their Points of Excellence, and how to obtain them. Illustrated. *In paper, price* 1s.

REPOUSSE WORK FOR AMATEURS: Being the Art of Ornamenting Thin Metal with Raised Figures. By L. L. HASLOPE. Illustrated. *In cloth gilt, price* 2s. 6d.

ROSES FOR AMATEURS. A Practical Guide to the Selection and Cultivation of the best Roses, both for Exhibition or mere Pleasure, by that large section of the Gardening World, the Amateur Lover of Roses. Illustrated. By the REV. J. HONYWOOD D'OMBRAIN, Hon. Sec. of the National Rose Society. *Price* 1s.

⁎ **All Books Post Free.**

ST. BERNARD, THE. Its History, Points, Breeding, and Rearing. By HUGH DALZIEL. Illustrated. *Demy 8vo, cloth, price* 2s. 6d.

SEA-FISHING FOR AMATEURS. Practical Instructions to Visitors at Seaside Places for Catching Sea-Fish from Pier-heads, Shore, or Boats, principally by means of Hand Lines, with a very useful List of Fishing Stations, the Fish to be caught there, and the Best Seasons. By FRANK HUDSON. Illustrated. *Crown 8vo, price* 1s.

SEASIDE WATERING PLACES. A Description of nearly 200 Holiday Resorts on the Coasts of England and Wales, the Channel Islands, and the Isle of Man, including the gayest and most quiet places, giving full particulars of them and their attractions, and all other information likely to assist persons in selecting places in which to spend their Holidays according to their individual tastes; with BUSINESS DIRECTORY of Tradesmen, arranged in order of the Towns. Sixth Edition. Illustrated. *In cloth, price* 2s. 6d.

SHEET METAL, WORKING IN: Being Practical Instructions for Making and Mending Small Articles in Tin, Copper, Iron, Zinc, and Brass. Illustrated. Third Edition. By the Rev. J. LUKIN, B.A. *In paper, price* 6d.

SHORTHAND, ON GURNEY'S SYSTEM (IMPROVED), LESSONS IN: Being Instructions in the Art of Shorthand Writing as used in the Service of the two Houses of Parliament. By R. E. MILLER. *In paper, price* 1s.

SHORTHAND, EXERCISES IN, ON GURNEY'S SYSTEM (IMPROVED): Being Shorthand without Study or Trouble; Illustrated Step by Step. A Sequel to "Lessons in Shorthand." By R. E. MILLER. *Price* 1s.

SHORTHAND SYSTEMS; WHICH IS THE BEST? Being a Discussion, by various Experts, on the Merits and Demerits of all the principal Systems, with Illustrative Examples. Edited by THOMAS ANDERSON. *In paper, price* 1s.

SICK NURSING AT HOME: Being Plain Directions and Hints for the Proper Nursing of Sick Persons, and the Home Treatment of Diseases and Accidents in case of Sudden Emergencies. By S. F. A. CAULFEILD. *In paper, price* 1s.; *in cloth, price* 1s. 6d.

SLEIGHT OF HAND. A Practical Manual of Legerdemain for Amateurs and Others. New Edition, Revised and Enlarged. Profusely Illustrated. By E. SACHS. *Cloth gilt, price* 6s. 6d.

SNAKES, MARSUPIALS, AND BIRDS. A Charming Book of Anecdotes, Adventures, and Zoological Notes relating to Snakes, Marsupials, and Birds. A capital Book for Boys, and all interested in Popular Natural History. By ARTHUR NICOLS, F.G.S., F.R.G.S., &c. Illustrated. *Price* 5s.

✱ **All Books Post Free.**

TAXIDERMY, PRACTICAL. A Manual of Instruction to the Amateur in Collecting, Preserving, and Setting-up Natural History Specimens of all kinds. Fully Illustrated with Examples and Working Diagrams. By MONTAGU BROWNE, F.Z.S., Curator of Leicester Museum. Second Edition. *In cloth gilt, price 7s. 6d.*

TOURIST'S ROUTE MAP of England and Wales. The Third Edition; thoroughly Revised. Shows clearly all the Main, and most of the Cross, Roads, and the Distances between the Chief Towns, as well as the Mileage from London. In addition to this, Routes of *Thirty of the most Interesting Tours* are printed in red. The Map is mounted on linen, and is the fullest, handiest, and best tourist's map in the market. *In cloth, price 1s.*

TRAPPING, PRACTICAL: Being some Papers on Traps and Trapping for Vermin, with a Chapter on General Bird Trapping and Snaring. By W. CARNEGIE. *In paper, price 1s.*

TURNING FOR AMATEURS: Being Descriptions of the Lathe and its Attachments and Tools, with Minute Instructions for their Effective Use on Wood, Metal, Ivory, and other Materials. New Edition, Revised and Enlarged. By JAMES LUKIN, B.A. Illustrated with 144 Engravings. *In cloth gilt, price 2s. 6d.*

TURNING LATHES. A Manual for Technical Schools and Apprentices. A Guide to Turning, Screw-cutting, Metal-Spinning, &c. Edited by JAMES LUKIN, B.A. Third Edition. With 194 Illustrations. *In cloth gilt, price 2s. 6d.*

VEGETABLE CULTURE FOR AMATEURS. Containing Concise Directions for the Cultivation of Vegetables in Small Gardens so as to insure Good Crops. With Lists of the Best Varieties of each Sort. By W. J. MAY. Illustrated. *Illustrated Wrapper, price 1s.*

VINE CULTURE FOR AMATEURS: Being Plain Directions for the Successful Growing of Grapes with the Means and Appliances usually at the command of Amateurs. Illustrated. Grapes are so generally grown in villa greenhouses that this book cannot fail to be of great service to many persons. By W. J. MAY. *In paper, price 1s.*

VIOLIN SCHOOL, PRACTICAL, for Home Students. A Practical Book of Instructions and Exercises in Violin Playing, for the use of Amateurs, Self-learners, Teachers, and others With a Supplement on "Easy Legato Studies for the Violin." By J. M. FLEMING. 1 *handsome vol., demy 4to, half Persian, price 9s. 6d.* Without Supplement, *price 7s. 6d.*

WAR MEDALS AND DECORATIONS, BRITISH. A Manual for Collectors and for all who are interested in the Achievements of the British Army and Navy, and the Rewards issued in public recognition of them; with some account of Civil Rewards for Valour. Beautifully Illustrated. *Price 7s. 6d.*

⁂ All Books Post Free.

Published by L. UPCOTT GILL, 170, Strand, London, W.C.

WATERING PLACES OF FRANCE, NORTHERN. A Guide for English People to the Holiday Resorts on the Coasts of the French Netherlands, Picardy, Normandy, and Brittany. By ROSA BAUGHAN. *In paper, price* 2s.

WOOD CARVING FOR AMATEURS. Containing Descriptions of all the requisite Tools, and Full Instructions for their Use in producing different varieties of Carvings. Illustrated. A book of very complete instructions for the amateur wood carver. *In paper, price* 1s.

London: L. UPCOTT GILL, 170, Strand, W.C.

Crown 8vo, cloth, with Illustrations, Price 5s.

WORKSHOP RECEIPTS,
FOR THE USE OF MANUFACTURERS, MECHANICS, AND SCIENTIFIC AMATEURS.
By ERNEST SPON.

Crown 8vo, cloth, 5s.

WORKSHOP RECEIPTS
(SECOND SERIES).
By ROBERT HALDANE.

Devoted mainly to subjects connected with Chemical Manufactures. An entirely New Volume. Uniform in Size, Style, and Type with the Original "Workshop Receipts."

Crown 8vo, cloth, 5s.

WORKSHOP RECEIPTS
(THIRD SERIES).
By C. G. WARNFORD LOCK, F.L.S.
Devoted mainly to Electrical and Metallurgical Subjects.

Crown 8vo, cloth, 5s.

WORKSHOP RECEIPTS
(FOURTH SERIES).
By C. G. WARNFORD LOCK, F.L.S.
Devoted mainly to Handicrafts and Mechanical Subjects.
250 *Illustrations, with Complete Index, and a General Index to the Four Series.*

Demy 8vo, cloth, 6s.

SPONS' MECHANIC'S OWN BOOK:
A Manual for Handicraftsmen and Amateurs, complete in one large vol., containing 700pp. and 1420 Illustrations. Second Edition.

CONTENTS:

Mechanical Drawing; Casting and Founding in Iron, Brass, Bronze, and other Alloys; Forging and Finishing Iron; Sheet-metal Working; Soldering, Brazing, and Burning; Carpentry and Joinery, embracing descriptions of some 400 Woods, over 200 Illustrations of Tools and their Uses, Explanations (with Diagrams) of 116 Joints and Hinges, and Details of Construction of Workshop Appliances, Rough Furniture Garden and Yard Erections, and House-Building; Cabinet-Making and Veneering; Carving and Fretcutting; Upholstery; Painting, Graining, and Marbling; Staining Furniture, Woods, Floors, and Fittings; Gilding, Dead and Bright, on various grounds; Polishing Marble, Metals, and Wood; Varnishing; Mechanical Movements, illustrating contrivances for transmitting Motion; Turning in Wood and Metals; Masonry, embracing Stonework, Brickwork, Terra-cotta, and Concrete; Roofing with Thatch, Tiles, Slates, Felt, Zinc, etc.; Glazing with and without Putty, and Lead Glazing; Plastering and Whitewashing; Paperhanging; Gas-fitting; Bell-hanging, ordinary and electric systems; Lighting; Warming; Ventilating; Roads, Pavements, and Bridges; Hedges, Ditches, and Drains; Water Supply and Sanitation; Hints on House Construction suited to New Countries.

London: E. & F. N. SPON, 125, Strand.

BOOKS PUBLISHED BY HORACE COX,

AT THE "FIELD" OFFICE, 346, STRAND, LONDON, W.C.

FOURTH EDITION. *In post 8vo, limp cloth, gilt, price 2s. 6d., by post 2s. 8d.*

THE ART OF SKATING; With Illustrations, Diagrams, and Plain Directions for the Acquirement of the Most Difficult and Graceful Movements. By GEORGE ANDERSON ("Cyclos"), Vice-President of the Crystal Palace Skating Club, and for many years President of the Glasgow Skating Club.

THIRD EDITION. *Price 7s. 6d., by post 7s. 10d.*

FIGURE SKATING; Being the Theory and Practice of the Art as Developed in England, with a Glance at its Origin and History. By H. C. VANDERVELL and T. MAXWELL WITHAM (Members of the London Skating Club). There are thousands of skaters who attain a small amount of skill in Figure Skating, and there stop, because they neither know what to do, or how to do it. A reference to this, the acknowledged Text Book of Figure Skating, will solve any difficulty that may have stopped progress for years. It now includes all the new Figures, with the new nomenclature which has been authorised by the Skating Club.

Price 8d., by post 9d.

THE "FIELD" LAWN TENNIS UMPIRES' SCORE-SHEET BOOK (Sixty Sets), with Instructions for the Use of Umpires. Adapted for the Use of Umpires, as used at the Championship Meetings.

FOURTH EDITION. *In demy 4to, on toned paper, and in fancy cover, price 2s., by post 2s. 2d.*

THE BOOK OF DINNER SERVIETTES contains a New Introduction on the Decoration of Dinner Tables, and General Directions for Folding the Serviettes. There are Twenty-one different kinds given, with Ninety-two Woodcuts illustrative of the various Folds required and the Serviettes complete.

Demy 8vo, price 5s. 6d., by post 5s. 10d.

THE ROTHAMSTED EXPERIMENTS ON THE GROWTH OF WHEAT BARLEY, AND THE MIXED HERBAGE OF GRASS LAND. By WILLIAM FREAM, B.Sc. Lond., F.L.S., F.G.S., F.S.S.

In demy 8vo, price 3s. 6d., by post 3s. 9d.

HINTS ON THE MANAGEMENT OF HAWKS. By J. E. HARTING, Author of "A Handbook of British Birds," "Essays on Sport and Natural History."

Price 1s., by post 1s. 2d. With Full-Page Coloured Illustration and Woodcuts.

PALLAS'S SAND GROUSE: Its Natural History, and a Plea for its Preservation. By W. B. TEGETMEIER.

THE RULES OF PIGEON SHOOTING. Published by Special Permission; the Hurlingham Club and the Gun Club Rules of Pigeon Shooting. SECOND EDITION. Bound together in cloth, gilt edges, price 6d., by post 7d.

THE LAWS OF LAWN TENNIS, as adopted by the Marylebone Cricket Club and the All England Croquet and Lawn Tennis Club. Entered at Stationers' Hall. Price 6d., by post 6½d.

"FIELD" OFFICE,
346, STRAND, LONDON, W.C.

SOME BOOKS FOR ANGLERS

PUBLISHED BY

SAMPSON LOW, MARSTON AND CO.

WALTON AND COTTON'S COMPLEAT ANGLER.

The Lea and Dove Illustrated Edition. Being the One Hundredth Edition of Walton and Cotton's ever-popular work, "The Compleat Angler." Edited, with Lives of Walton and Cotton, by R. B. MARSTON, Editor of the *Fishing Gazette*, Hon. Treasurer of the Fly Fishers' Club, &c., and containing a Reprint (by permission) of "The Chronicle of the Compleat Angler," being a Bibliographical Record of its various Editions and imitations. By THOMAS WESTWOOD and THOMAS SATCHELL. The principal feature of this Edition will be a set of fifty-four Full-page Photogravures, printed from Copper Plates, on fine plate paper, of Views on the Lea, Dove, &c.

EDITION DE LUXE, in 2 vols., royal 4to, each copy numbered and signed, to Subscribers £10 10s. nett.

The DEMY QUARTO EDITION, bound in half morocco, gilt top, £5 5s. nett.

"The noblest gift-book that has been issued for many years."—*St. James' Gazette*.

"Never has Walton been more honoured. . . . Among collectors, therefore, there is no question but that the book will be attractive. It will be one of the forms in which the work of Walton will be most coveted."—*Standard*.

"These sumptuous volumes."—*Spectator*. "A truly magnificent edition."—*Field*. "This noble edition."—*Daily News*.

READY IN THE SPRING.

DRY FLY FISHING IN THEORY AND PRACTICE.

By FREDERIC M. HALFORD, F.L.S., Author of "Floating Flies and How to Dress Them," "Detached Badger" of the *Field*, Member of the "Houghton Club," "Fly Fishers' Club," &c. An *Edition de Luxe*, limited to 100 copies, and the First Edition of 500 copies, are in preparation, and will be published this season. Illustrated with Plates showing the Position of the Rod and Line in making various Casts used in Dry Fly Fishing; also Coloured and other Plates, giving the Life History of the Mayfly; a Coloured Plan showing how the Weeds in a River should be Cut, &c., &c.

CONDITIONS OF PUBLICATION.

Edition de Luxe, imperial octavo, printed on the best English hand made paper, bound in full morocco, with gilt top, with the plates on mounts. Limited strictly to 100 copies. *Each copy will be numbered and signed*. Price per copy. Subscribers, £2 5s.

First Edition, royal octavo, printed on the finest printing paper, cloth extra, 500 copies. Price per copy, Subscribers, £1 5s.

N.B.—All Coloured Illustrations are hand-coloured in both Editions, except the plans illustrating Chapters IV. and XIII.

FLOATING FLIES AND HOW TO DRESS THEM. A

Treatise on the most Modern Methods of Dressing Artificial Flies for Trout and Grayling. With full illustrated Directions, and containing ninety Hand-coloured Engravings of the most Killing Patterns, together with a few Hints to Dry-fly Fishermen. By FREDERIC M. HALFORD, "Detached Badger" of *The Field*, Member of the Houghton Club, Fly-fishers' Club, &c. Second edition, demy 8vo, cloth, 15s., post free.

> "Of Blue Duns and Bumbles, of hooks and their eyes,
> Of Red Tags and Coachmen, and all sorts of flies:
> Of Wickhams, Red Spinners, and others, ne'er failing
> To lure out of water the trout and the grayling—
> Here Halford discourses, and shows a collection
> Of ninety fly-portraits, all limned to perfection:
> A capital volume, and no one will doubt it,
> No fisherman now should be ever without it!"—*Punch*.

NEAR AND FAR: an Angler's Sketches of Home Sport and

COLONIAL LIFE. By WM. SENIOR ("Red Spinner"), Angling Editor of *The Field*, Author of "Waterside Sketches," &c. Crown 8vo, cloth, 6s.

"The author is not merely an expert all-round angler, but is an all-round lover of nature; and he has the very happy faculty of knowing how to describe what he sees and what he has done. He has fished, and shot, and hunted, and communed with nature the world over; and he describes his adventures with a lightness and brightness of touch which to anyone who has in him the least love of nature cannot but be irresistibly charming."—*Fishing Gazette*.

TO ANGLERS.—If you do not know the paper, send a post-card to the Manager of THE FISHING GAZETTE, St. Dunstan's House, Fetter Lane, London.

TO ANGLERS.—"The Fishing Gazette"

is Devoted entirely to Angling, and gives, every Saturday, Original Articles, Reports from Rivers, Clubs, Correspondence; and has a Splendid Show of Advertisements from leading Fishing Tackle Makers, Fishing Hotels, &c.

TO ANGLERS.—Send or a LIST OF BOOKS ON ALL KINDS OF ANGLING to Manager of THE FISHING GAZETTE, St. Dunstan's House, Fetter Lane, London.

ROWLANDS' TOILET ARTICLES

Have been known for nearly 100 years to be the best which can be obtained; the best articles are, in the long run, always the cheapest.

ROWLANDS' MACASSAR OIL

Is the best and safest preserver and beautifier of the hair, and has a most delicate and fragrant bouquet. It contains no lead or mineral ingredients, and can also be had in

A GOLDEN COLOUR

for fair and golden-haired children, and people whose hair has become grey. Sizes: 3/6, 7/-; 10/6, equal to four small.

ROWLANDS' KALYDOR

Is a most soothing emollient and refreshing preparation for the face, hands, and arms. It removes all freckles, tan, sunburn, sting of insects, prickly heat, chaps, redness, irritation and roughness of the skin, &c., produces a beautiful and delicate complexion, and renders the

SKIN SOFT, FAIR,

and delicate; it is warranted free from any greasy or metallic ingredients. Sizes 4/6 and 8/6. *Half-sized bottles at 2/3.*

ROWLANDS' ODONTO

Is the best, purest, and most fragrant Tooth Powder; it prevents and arrests decay, strengthens the gums, gives a pleasing fragrance to the breath, and renders the

TEETH WHITE AND SOUND.

ROWLANDS' EUKONIA

Is a pure and delicate toilet powder, free from any bismuth or metallic ingredients Sold in three tints, white, rose, and cream, 2/6 per box. Ask for

ROWLANDS' ARTICLES,

of 20, HATTON GARDEN, LONDON, and avoid cheap, spurious imitations, under the same or similar names.

BY SPECIAL APPOINTMENT.

Purveyors by Special Warrants to
H.M. THE QUEEN
and
H.R.H. THE PRINCE OF WALES.

BY SPECIAL APPOINTMENT.

SPRATTS PATENT
Meat "Fibrine" Vegetable
DOG CAKES
(WITH BEETROOT).

BEWARE OF WORTHLESS IMITATIONS!
SEE EACH CAKE IS STAMPED
SPRATTS PATENT and a "X."

COD LIVER OIL
DOG CAKES.
For Puppies after Distemper, and for Dainty Feeders and Sick or Pet Dogs.

DISTEMPER POWDERS, WORM POWDERS, MANGE, ECZEMA, and EAR CANKER LOTIONS, TONIC CONDITION PILLS, &c.

PAMPHLET ON CANINE DISEASES,
And full List of Medicines, Post Free.

Dog, Poultry, and Game Houses and Appliances.

TO POULTRY REARERS.

SPRATTS PATENT
POULTRY MEAL.
The Most Nutritious and Digestible Food for Chicks and Laying Hens (being thoroughly cooked). Samples Post Free.

New Edition of "THE COMMON SENSE of POULTRY KEEPING," 3d., Post Free

GRANULATED PRAIRIE MEAT, "CRISSEL."
Price 25s. per cwt. Takes the Place of Insect Life.

"CARDIAC;" A TONIC FOR POULTRY.
Price 1s. per Packet, or 3s. per 7lb. Bag.

GAME MEAL.
SAMPLE AND FULL PARTICULARS POST FREE.

Extract from "THE FIELD":—"Thanks to Spratts Pheasant Meal and Crissel, I have reduced the cost a great deal, and reared a considerably greater average With Spratts Food they require no custards, ants' eggs, or, in fact, anything from hatching till they are turned in coverts and eat corn."—CAREFUL SPORTSMAN.

"The Common Sense of Pheasant Rearing," 3d., Post Free.

Spratts Patent, Limited, London, S.E.

Webster Family Library of Veterinary Medicine
Cu...
T...
20...
North Grafton, MA 01536

CPSIA information can be obtained
at www.ICGtesting.com
Printed in the USA
LVHW081536010822
724888LV00010B/403